Dumaine's Amoskeag:
Let the Record Speak

Arthur M. Kenison, Ph.D.

FREDERIC C. DUMAINE

DUMAINE'S AMOSKEAG:
LET THE RECORD SPEAK

ARTHUR M. KENISON, PH.D.

PUBLISHED BY SAINT ANSELM COLLEGE PRESS
MANCHESTER, NEW HAMPSHIRE

Published by Saint Anselm College Press

100 Saint Anselm Drive

Manchester, NH 03102-1310

Printed and bound in the United States of America.

October 1997

First Edition

Library of Congress Cataloging-in-Publication Data

Dumaine's Amoskeag: Let The Record Speak / Arthur M. Kenison
    Includes bibliographical references and index.
    ISBN 0-9629547-1-3 (alk. paper)
    1. Economics —United States.   2. Education, Higher—
United States—Economics.   I. Kenison, Arthur M.
II. Saint Anselm College Press   CIP

On the personal side, to Jeanne, who has had to
read this book too often, and to Tracy, Dale and Dan, who will
now feel obliged to read the book once.

On the public side, to the laborers,
managers and owners who united to make the
Amoskeag Manufacturing Company
a great organization.

On the professional side, to all my students,
particularly those who understood the
nobility of Dumaine's efforts.

CONTENTS

PREFACE

As a young man growing up in Manchester in the 1950's, I was well schooled in the folklore of the Amoskeag Manufacturing Company, the world's largest cotton textile manufacturer, and how under the leadership of Frederic Dumaine it deserted the City of Manchester during the Great Depression in the 1930's. The consensus held by those old enough to have been affected by the closing was that the absentee control in Boston, suffering from giantism and a lack of concern for the city, was the primary cause of the liquidation. To this day, critics continue to point out the insensitivity of Dumaine in selecting Christmas Eve 1935 as the day to close the mills for the last time. (In reality the mills were closed the previous September. The misconception on the December 24 date stems from the fact that this was the day Amoskeag notified its bondholders that the bonds were in default and the company was seeking protection under the bankruptcy laws with the intention of reorganizing and reopening manufacturing in the near future.) Legend goes on to expound how local citizens formed Amoskeag Industries, which salvaged the manufacturing facilities abandoned by the Boston-based company and saved the city from economic disaster. This view is held not only by many of the residents of Manchester, but also by historians and economists who seemingly studied the closing.

During the spring of 1989, while on sabbatical from my teaching duties at Saint Anselm College, I took the opportunity to study the financial and economic factors that led to the bankruptcy of the Amoskeag Manufacturing Company. My findings led me to a substantially different interpretation of the events leading to the closing of the mills than that held by the citizens of Manchester, as well as by those historians and economists who have studied Amoskeag.

After the closing, many of the workers who lost their jobs said they felt that Amoskeag's stockholders had no right to remove the retained earnings that had been built up over the previous hundred years. They said they believed the money should have been used to combat the hard times the textile industry was experiencing. They had expected the company to continue operating at a loss to insure their employment. Others simply did not believe that the Amoskeag was in reality losing money.

I spoke to an audience of retired Manchester residents. While many there were too young to have been working in the mills before the closing, most could remember the impact on their families. For the first time, I was reasonably successful in explaining the position of the stockholders by posing to the audience this less-than-perfect analogy:

> Assume that you had deposited money in a local bank some ten years ago. Assume further that over that ten-year period you earned a substantially higher interest rate than in other banks in the community. Finally, assume that the bank notifies you that if you keep your money in the bank over the next several years, you would not earn any interest but instead you could expect to see your account balance reduced by five percent per year. Would you keep your money in the bank or withdraw the current balance and deposit it in an alternative bank where you could expect to earn a fair return?

As you would expect, the audience was unanimous: They would withdraw their money. When I pointed out the similar motivation of stockholders when they decide to liquidate a business, the audience began to appreciate the position of the owners of capital.

While the directors of the corporation had a moral duty to obey the law and treat their workers fairly, they also had a moral obligation to act as trustees of the shareholders' investment. The management could not unilaterally decide to take unwarranted risks with the corporation's capital merely to keep the workers employed. The directors had a moral and legal obligation to use prudence in the management of whatever profits were left over after paying the costs of production. If estimated future returns from the reinvestment of these profits were not adequate, the directors had an obligation to distribute the funds to the stockholders.

What I had expected to find in my study was a well managed, relatively socially responsible corporation, forced to close by insurmountable wage differences between the North and the South. While my assumption as to the financial factors leading to the eventual bankruptcy of the Amoskeag Manufacturing Company proved to be correct, I was amazed to find how incorrectly history has interpreted Amoskeag's social conscience. My investigation leads me to conclude that the performance of F.C. Dumaine in particular and the management of Amoskeag Manufacturing Company in general serve as excellent examples of the difficulties facing a corporation attempting to balance its fiduciary responsibility to its shareholders with its social responsibility to its employees and its host community. In fact, if Dumaine were to be criticized at all, it should be that his devotion to the City of Manchester and its workers caused him to lean too far in the direction of social responsibility at the cost of his own and other shareholders' personal wealth.

The majority of my sabbatical research was devoted to examining the corporate records of Amoskeag and its auxiliary industries and to review the personal files of F.C. Dumaine. In addition, I studied the various works of critics of Amoskeag that were written shortly after the bankruptcy.

Toward the end of my sabbatical, I met with F.C. Dumaine, Jr., eldest son of F.C. Dumaine and immediate successor as chief executive officer of the Amoskeag Co., the Boston-based holding company that controlled Amoskeag Manufacturing Company. I met a man not interested in making excuses but one earnestly willing to let the record speak for itself. The man I met was the son of a man whom I had come to know and respect through my research. While I have serious concern for the potential inaccuracy of oral history, I was compelled to do further research based on two points that arose in our conversation.

The first point was his response to my question about why Amoskeag continued to expand its capacity and employment in Manchester in the twentieth century since corporate records indicated that the firm was well aware of the competitive advantages of Southern plants. His initial response was to pass off the question and change the subject. I would have expected the same response from his father: In effect, let the facts speak for themselves. At the risk of pressing his hospitality, I restated my original question. "Since your father was well aware of the labor cost advantage of manufacturing in the South, why did he build the Coolidge Mill in 1909?"

He became silent. Contemplative. Reflective. He looked me in the eye, and said, "Because Dad loved Manchester."

The second point relates to a car trip he and his father made to Manchester in 1936 when the senior Dumaine was trying to financially reorganize the Amoskeag Manufacturing Company to reopen the mills in Manchester. According to F.C., Jr., his father had driven from Boston for F.C. to meet with a group of New Hampshire bondholders key to the success of the reorganization plan presented by Amoskeag. Parking the car on Hanover Street. F.C., Jr. remained in the car while F.C. went into the Amoskeag Bank Building to meet with bondholders in an office above the bank.

When F.C. returned to the car not a word was spoken for the first half of the trip back to Massachusetts. Finally F.C., Jr. broke the silence. F.C. was furious. The majority of Manchester's bondholders had decided not to support the reorganization plan, he told his son. He said the Manchester bondholders prior to the meeting had given their word to go along with the refinancing to keep the mills open. He said he reminded them of the commitment. They argued that they only said they *might* go along with the reorganization. The following day the trustees of Amoskeag withdrew their reorganization plan because it did not have the backing of the Manchester community.

At this point I remembered having seen a series of letters between Amoskeag and Manchester bondholders in my previous review of the Dumaine files. When I had originally come across the letters, I gave them little attention since they were not directly related to my study of the economic factors leading to the loss in competitiveness with the South. However, I knew that the correspondence would be critical to my current work on Dumaine's stewardship of the Amoskeag Manufacturing Company in the twentieth century.

Having completed my research on the economic and financial factors leading to the closing of the Amoskeag and having exhausted my sabbatical time, I began the slower task of reconstructing the history of Amoskeag under Frederic Dumaine. Shortly thereafter I came across a rough draft of the history of Amoskeag in the twentieth century.[1] Sadly, the author is unknown. Two possible authors are Professor Charles Coulter of New Hampshire University (now the University of New Hampshire in Durham), and Professor Charles Moore of Harvard University. Both names appear in Dumaine's diary as individuals who were approached in 1939 to write an updated history of Amoskeag in 1939. It seems unlikely that Coulter would have been the author because he was one of two researchers commissioned by the WPA to look into factors leading to the closing of Amoskeag.[2] While he would have the advantage of having previously researched the subject, the conclusions of the writer of the unpublished history are significantly different than those found in the WPA study. Two Manchester individuals often cited as potential writers are Bill McKay, the former head of the print shop at Amoskeag and a frequent writer for the Amoskeag Bulletin, the company newsletter, and Fred Lamb, a former Amoskeag employee who became the first curator of the Manchester Historic Association. One final candidate would be a person with the last name of Wayman, whose "Typescript Notes from the Dumaine's Diary" I found in the Dumaine files.[3]

The history was written some fifty years ago and was to have been an update of a previous history compiled by George Waldo Brown and printed and bound in the mills of the Amoskeag Manufacturing Company in 1915.[4] The draft of this later history covers the Amoskeag Manufacturing Company through 1931. The manuscript also treated the history of the Amoskeag Company, the Boston based holding company after that date. However, the chapter dealing with years between 1931 and the bankruptcy was either lost, destroyed, or never written.

To a great extent, this book owes its existence to that unpublished work as one of the primary sources of historical information. Much of the unpublished work has been incorporated directly into this book. The reader, however, should not attribute the interpretations and conclusions in this book to that unknown writer because that work was written only to chronicle events.

This book provides an analysis of factors leading to the demise of the Amoskeag Manufacturing Company as a case study in the difficulty of balancing the corporation's responsibilities to its stockholders with its obligations to its workers and host community.

As with most authors, I am indebted to many. First and foremost is the unknown author of the history. Without such an effort, the historical background could not have been reconstructed. Of near equal importance is Mrs. Elizabeth Lessard, who has devoted a major portion of her life to the preservation of Manchester history through her work as librarian of the Manchester Historic Association. She has been an invaluable resource in seeking additional information and in providing me guidance in research. Next I would like to express my appreciation to many of my colleagues at Saint Anselm College, whose helpful suggestions have contributed to the improvement of the manuscript. In particular I wish to thank Professors Vincent Capowski, David George, Christopher Hamel, Robert Perreault, John Romps, Joseph Spoerl and Kenneth Walker. I wish to thank Eileen Chandonnet and Marianne Lake for their careful reading and insightful questions about the work. I also am indebted to my colleague and wife Professor Jeanne Kenison, who never seems to have tired of listening and advising me on this manuscript.

As is the usual practice, I will accept the responsibility for all errors in the work. In a somewhat unusual practice, I must add the caveat that the opinions expressed in the interpretation of the facts are those of the current writer, and do not necessarily reflect the views of the unknown author of the original history, Mrs. Lessard, or the colleagues I have mentioned.

Arthur M. Kenison
February 1996

POSTSCRIPT

On May 3, 1997, I attended a memorial service for Frederic C. "Buck" Dumaine, Jr. At that time, I delivered copies of my manuscript to Buck's three children, and I had the good fortune to talk with Dudley Dumaine, one of Buck's sons, for some time. While I did expect a note of appreciation for the copies of my manuscript, I was humbled to receive a letter from Dudley offering, on behalf of the third generation of Dumaines, to provide me with personal material, family members' recollections, and to fund the publication of this book. Dudley's letter in part stated:

> Amoskeag's emotional historical distortions have contributed to the current discreditization of respect the American people have for the honorable driving forces that made America what it is. We also understand that we, the descendants of F.C. Dumaine, Sr., are subject to the same errors of oral history within ourselves, as did the labor force of Amoskeag, and for the same reason; lack of full information.

The letter went on to state that this additional information was for my "...analysis, inclusion, modification and/or rejection."

Subsequently, Dudley Dumaine provided me with three basic categories of material; oral history, personal Dumaine files and galley proofs of a book-in-progress titled *Dumaine of New England*.[1]

In the 1950's, the Dumaine family had contracted with the late Dorothy G. Wayman, a retired Boston Globe reporter and biographer, to write a book based on Dumaine's diaries. Wayman was noted above as a potential author of the unpublished history of Amoskeag. After three years of work on the biography and for reasons unknown, the family decided against the publication.

I found little in the book relative to Amoskeag that I had not already discovered. There was, however, much written confirming my prior opinion on the measure of the man. Of particular interest to test my already decided conclusions about Dumaines' motivations is her review of F.C.'s actions in controlling Waltham Watch, a subject not covered in my book but in itself a fascinating study. At one point she writes:

> Dumaine's human side appears in an incident in 1937, when a young man attempting to move a pan filled with gasoline was fatally burned. [Quoting his Diary she goes on to state]

> Thursday, July 22, 1937: **** of the **** Insurance Company called to discuss the John Kempton case. I explained to him unless he was willing to pay the family $3,000, with $150 towards funeral expenses and the nurses bill, $256, in view of the great suffering and unusual circumstances, I could not recommend a settlement on no other basis and should insist the case be put up to the Industrial Accident Board.

> He pointed out the question of willful negligence on the company's part might be raised if the question went before the Board and the watch company might be held for half the damages. I told him I cared nothing about that. If it could be shown willful negligence existed, the watch company should be penalized. I could see no other solution and did not care to horse-trade.[2]

In a second incident relating the time when Dumaine was retired from control of Waltham Watch she states:

> On May 22, 1944, the Waltham News-Tribune printed a tribute to Dumaine and his record of achievement and also printed a long list of names of Waltham employees of twenty years' service or more, who had received unspecified bonuses. The public supposed that these have been paid by the company, as originally authorized by vote of the directors and mentioned in Dumaine's diary. Actually because government consent could not be procured, in the end Dumaine footed the entire bill from his own pocket.[3]

Wayman concludes her chapter on Waltham Watch with the following comment:

> It is obvious that the $125,000 of bread Dumaine cast upon the waters in 1923, at Waltham, twenty years later came back in the form of a loaf of about a million dollars in cash. A quarter of it he paid to the United States government in taxes, and one third he had donated in bonuses to the veteran watchmakers. Money, however, was not Dumaine's objective or the mainspring to his operations. . .
>
> His satisfaction and his pride in the success of his endeavors at Waltham, as in Bay State Fishing Company or Fore River Ship and Engine Company or Agwilines, was to see the American economy and industry "working right," clear of debt, giving employment to workers, prosperity to the community, a reasonable return on risk capital.[4]

One final point in the Wayman manuscript substantiated my assumptions of Dumaine's attitude in letting the record speak for itself relates to a conversation and subsequent correspondence between Dumaine and F.D. Roosevelt. During the conversation with the president, Dumaine had quoted a saying of Abraham Lincoln's which Roosevelt had not heard. Upon returning to Boston, Dumaine had the quote printed, matted and framed and sent it to the president. The text and FDR's letter are on the following pages.

Lest the reader conclude that the book has been tainted by Dumaine's support in publication, let me emphatically state that all of the material that I have reviewed substantiated the conclusions reached in my research prior to the family's generous offer.

Because publication of the manuscript is funded by the Dumaine family, I have relinquished all rights to Saint Anselm College to permit all proceeds to establish a scholarship for descendants of Amoskeag employees who qualify to attend Saint Anselm College.

Arthur M. Kenison
October 1997

May 5, 1942.

Dear Fred:-

That is a mighty nice quotation and delightfully printed and framed. I am hanging it up in my office that all may read.

My best wishes to you,

Always sincerely,

Fred C. Dumaine, Esq.,
Sears Building,
Boston,
Massachusetts.

Amoskeag Millyard when times were flourishing

Chapter I

Introduction

In 1915 the Amoskeag Manufacturing Company, whose mills covered both sides of the Merrimack River in Manchester, N.H., was recognized as the largest cotton textile firm in the world. The company was known for the quality of its output, the efficiency of its production, its concern for its employees and the profitability for its stockholders. Frederic C. Dumaine, the treasurer and chief executive officer of the corporation, was one of the leading businessmen of his time. In the words of one writer:

> A mill that has done more for its workers will be hard to discover, and a plant that has faced competition and rewarded its stockholders as well is not readily found.[1]

By 1936, only twenty-one years later, the same firm was bankrupt. Amoskeag management was being severely criticized for inefficient production and failing to consider the welfare of its employees in its financial decision making. The irony of the situation was that Amoskeag's devotion to its employees was the cause of this turnabout.

Amoskeag, like all New England textile firms, was experiencing increasing competition from lower labor cost mills in the South. Unlike many of its contemporaries, Amoskeag decided it would not follow the obvious strategy of closing existing New England mills and concentrate production in the South. On the contrary, the firm had two major expansions in Manchester in this time period. The first was the construction of a new mill in 1909. The second was in 1922, when Amoskeag acquired the Manchester facilities of a national firm that decided to move all of its production to the lower labor cost South. Prior to either of these expansions, the corporate records indicated that the management was fully aware of the labor cost differences. However, the company took the position that it was and always would remain a Manchester company.

The history of the Amoskeag Manufacturing Company in the twentieth century provides the reader with an excellent case study of the difficulties and limitations of a corporation that attempts to balance its social responsibilities to its workers and host community with its fiduciary obligations to its stockholders. Rather than being praised for the attempt, the management in general and F. C. Dumaine in particular were criticized for lack of concern for the welfare of the workers.

One might well expect that the original reaction of the work force would be to blame the company for the situation. However, these feelings continued for many years, as demonstrated in the 1968 oral history on Amoskeag.[2] The following two quotes reflect the ill feelings still held by some former Amoskeag workers. One worker interviewed attacked Dumaine personally stating:

> When Frederic Dumaine went in as treasurer of the Company, he pocketed everything and left nothing for the others. He looked out only for himself, he didn't look out for the good of the company, so it couldn't last long being run like that.[3]

A second individual interviewed was hired in 1934, the year before the closing, to act as a troubleshooter with the goal of improving employee relations. He said:

> Labor knew as much about accounting as anybody else. The workers' argument to me was: "My grandmother and my grandfather worked hard to establish this surplus. We really earned it for Amoskeag Manufacturing Company. Now, in the Depression, why can't they at least pay me a living wage and keep the mill operating? That surplus is really ours, but they've taken it away.[4]

Economists, politicians and historians, critical of Amoskeag, blamed the closing on alternative forms of mismanagement. Arthur Black, the Bankruptcy Master in the Amoskeag case, and Harvard economist Alan R. Sweezy, cite Amoskeag's corporate restructuring in 1925 and 1927 as depleting the financial resources of the company at a time when these funds were necessary to cover short term losses.[5,6] This point is not substantially different from that held by the workers. U.S. Congressman Adolph J. Sabath attributed the problems to the issuing of watered-down securities associated with the refinancing.[7] Professors Daniel Creamer and Charles Coulter held that the practice of acquiring the assets of neighboring textile firms instead of purchasing new equipment made the company's equipment obsolete. They held that the failure to reinvest adequately in capital equipment in later years compounded the situation.[8] They also attributed Amoskeag's problems to failing to keep pace with changes in the marketplace. In particular, they were critical of the firm for staying with gingham production and for not expanding its pilot production of nylon. They further blamed the eventual decline on the loss of market share caused by the nine-month strike in 1922.

The feeling among professional writers on the subject has not changed much over the years. In a 1987 *Forbes* magazine article, Saunders writes:

> Dumaine came to be a despised man. He bled companies of working capital, starved their capital budgets, dumped loyal workers, slashed wages, and demanded more hours, all while enriching security holders, including himself.[9]

A 1993 feature in *Audacity* presented a similar conclusion:

> F.C. Dumaine shifted eighteen million dollars of the company's assets into a newly created holding company. The move protected the money but left the Amoskeag Manufacturing Company short of the cash needed for maintenance and modernization ... In 1935 the mills shut down, and the corporation filed bankruptcy court. The court refused the Amoskeag's application for reorganization and ordered liquidation. The demise of the Amoskeag tore the heart out of Manchester.[10]

All of the critics, both past and current, failed to see the inevitability of the closing once Amoskeag had determined to remain a New Hampshire firm. To understand this point, consider the following three sets of income statements for New England and Southern textile mills.

In the nineteenth century there was little production of textiles in the South since that area of the country lacked the waterpower necessary to serve as an energy source. The industry in New England could expect to have labor costs equal to about $40 for each $100 of sales. All other costs, including materials, overhead and energy, amounted to an additional $55. This left a $5 profit margin, which was sufficient to justify plant investments. Whenever increases in demand or other factors caused the profit margin to exceed the required $5 level, competitive forces would cause new or existing firms to expand output in search of the excess returns promised by the higher-than-necessary profit margin. These forces would continue until deteriorating market prices caused the profit margin to return to the normal $5 level. See the first set of income statements for the 1820-1880 time period.

When advances in coal-generated energy sources at the end of the nineteenth century enabled the South to enter textile manufacturing, it did so with a labor rate some 25 percent below the mills in the North. This would amount to $30 per $100 of sales rather than the $40 experienced in the North. While continual improvements in the utilization of water power, the advantage of a skilled labor force in New England and wartime profits counteracted the Southern labor cost advantage, over time the superiority of coal-generated energy, the equalization of labor skills, and the end of the war resulted in a situation where the Southern wage rate provided mill owners in that section of the country with the economic incentive of excess profits to increase output. The second set of income statements depict the economics facing the New England and the Southern mill in the 1880-1920 time period.

Since Southern mills were earning a $15 profit when only a $5 level was necessary, they responded by increasing capacity. While the Southern firms realized that their continual expansion of output would cause the price to drop, they knew that they would still earn a normal profit. On the other hand, as long as the South had a labor cost advantage, the North would face negative returns as depicted in the third set of income statements in the 1920 and later time period.

Comparison of
New England and Southern Textiles Mills

1820-1880

New England			Southern		
Sales	$100		Sales	XXX	
Expenses			Expenses		
Labor	$40		Labor	XX	
Other	55	95	Other	XX	XX
Profit (Loss)	$ 5		Profit (Loss)		X

1880-1920

New England			Southern		
Sales	$100		Sales	$100	
Expenses			Expenses		
Labor	$40		Labor	$30	
Other	55	95	Other	55	85
Profit (Loss)	$ 5		Profit (Loss)	$ 15	

1920-on

New England			Southern		
Sales	$ 90		Sales	$ 90	
Expenses			Expenses		
Labor	$40		Labor	$30	
Other	55	95	Other	55	85
Profit (Loss)	($ 5)		Profit (Loss)	$ 5	

Amoskeag could have insured its profitability into the twenty-first century had it relocated its mills to the South in the 1920's and 1930's, and the subsequent relocation to foreign countries in the 1970's and 1980's. However, this would not have preserved employment in Manchester. The true value of studying the history of Amoskeag is that it vividly demonstrates the limitations that a company faces when it attempts to establish a corporate social policy that is in conflict with the competitive markets.

This book attempts to illustrate the inevitability of this outcome by combining the historical research of the unknown author of the unpublished history cited in the preface with this author's economic interpretations of the facts.

Chapter II reveals the history of the corporation in the nineteenth century based on the first chapter of the unpublished history. The material provides useful insight into the philosophy of the corporation and the competitiveness of the textile industry. In particular, the reader should note that Amoskeag was well aware of the labor cost advantage of the South when it decided to build the Jefferson plant in Manchester in 1888.

Chapter III, based on the second chapter of the unpublished history, covers the expansion of capacity under Dumaine. The issue of growth through mergers versus internal construction of new plants is examined. We learn that both methods of expansion were used during this period and to assess whether acquisitions had a negative impact on Amoskeag's long-run competitiveness.

Chapters IV and V look at Amoskeag during its period of peak production and profitability. Chapter IV, covering the years 1911 to 1916, explores the time of maximum output and the introduction of many employee benefits that were quite innovative at the time. Chapter V, covering the years 1916 through 1921, illustrates the substantial profits earned during World War I. While these profits provided Amoskeag with the reserve to weather bad economic conditions, even greater profits were being earned by Southern textile firms. Since these Southern firms were well aware of their cost advantage, they were investing the profits into plant expansions despite their creation of national overcapacity. The firms in the South knew that their cost advantage would insure their success in increasing their output at the expense of the North. Chapters IV and V are based on the third and fourth chapters of the unpublished history.

To emphasize the impact of three significant events, the 1922 strike, the refinancing of 1925 and 1927, and the Great Depression, material in the fifth and sixth chapters of the unpublished history is broken into three chapters. Chapter VI — 1922 through 1924 — concentrates on the strike and the immediate post-strike years. Particular attention is devoted to management's rationale in announcing the wage cut and increase in work week, the cause for the workers to go on strike. In effect, while Amoskeag would have preferred to see Southern wages rise to the level in the North, wage equalization was essential for long term survival in Manchester.

Chapter VII examines the financial restructuring during 1925 and 1927, often cited as evidence of Amoskeag's structured liquidation of its investments in Manchester. This chapter provides an alternative interpretation of Amoskeag's motives in this period. The restructuring of 1925 is presented as attempts to put to rest stockholders' fear that the management would deplete past accumulated earnings through a continual operation at a loss. The refinancing of 1927 is depicted as a reaction to corporate raiders eager to purchase Amoskeag to close the mill and sell the assets for quick financial gain. Amoskeag was attempting to balance it obligations to its workers with its fiduciary responsibility to its shareholders.

Chapter VIII, based on material in the sixth chapter of the unpublished history, examines the difficulties that Amoskeag experienced during the Depression. Of particular interest is the continuing attempt on the part of management to seek parity in wage rates with the South. What should have been Amoskeag's plant and equipment investment philosophy during that period is addressed.

Chapters IX and X are based on this author's review of the corporate records and Dumaine's files. Chapter IX focuses on the years from 1932 to the final liquidation of the Amoskeag Manufacturing Company in 1936 and chronicles the attempts by Dumaine to reorganize with the goal of restarting production in Manchester. Chapter X examines the critics of Dumaine's management and summarizes conclusions reached throughout this book.

While this is a book about Amoskeag and the textile industry almost a century ago, it provides new insights into contemporary American industries' attempt to regain a competitive edge in world markets. The reader will see the parallels between Amoskeag's efforts in the first quarter of this century and the down sizing and restructuring of Chrysler, Caterpillar, General Motors and International Business Machines in the last quarter of the same century. The most important point to be learned from a study of Amoskeag is that a corporation cannot succeed in accomplishing a socially desirable goal, valiant though it may be, when it is in direct opposition to the dictates of a competitive market.

AMOSKEAG FALLS

CHAPTER II

Amoskeag Before Dumaine

One could attribute three different years as the beginning of the Amoskeag Manufacturing Company's operations in Manchester, N.H. The first year, 1805, is the year that the first textile mill was built by Benjamin Prichard. The reason for selecting what would eventually become the City of Manchester as the site for the mill was the superb water power provided by the Amoskeag Falls of the Merrimack River. The original mill was constructed on the west side of the river on property that at that time was within the boundaries of the town of Goffstown, a portion that was subsequently annexed to the City of Manchester. The mill, later reorganized under the name of the Amoskeag Cotton & Wool Manufactory, was closed in 1815.

The second year acknowledged to be the beginning of the Amoskeag, 1825, is the year that the eventual incorporators of Amoskeag purchased the mills and began operation under the name of the Amoskeag Manufacturing Company. In that year three new owners — Samuel Slater, Larned Pitcher and Ira Gay — acquired the property. Three additional partners — Oliver Dean, Lyman Tiffany and Willard Sayles — were then brought into the business. The company was run as a partnership which by 1831 had three mills, two on the west side of the river and one on the island below the falls.

The third year, 1831, is legitimately attributed as the beginning of Amoskeag, when the six partners went through the process of having the business incorporated. On July 1, 1831, the corporate charter was granted by the New Hampshire House of Representatives. The charter was signed by Franklin Pierce, then speaker of the New Hampshire House and later president of the United States. The authorized capital was $1,000,000 made up of 1,000 shares of $1,000 par value. The New Hampshire House authorized the new corporation to:

> Establish, manage and carry on the manufacture of cotton and woolen, iron and other lawful manufacturing on or near Amoskeag Falls in Goffstown and any and all such branches of manufacture and trade as is necessary, and also to construct such dams, canals, mills, buildings, machines and works they deem necessary.

The company paid its first dividend of $60 on each par value of $1,000 in 1834. Two years later there were more than seventy different stockholders. Many of the names, such as Amory, Appleton, Gardner, Lawrence and Lowell, were noted for their textile holdings in Massachusetts. Two men who were primarily responsible for the success of Amoskeag in its formative years were its treasurer, William Amory, and its agent, Ezekiel A. Straw. Throughout most of Amoskeag Manufacturing Corporation's life, the treasurer operated out of a Boston office as the chief executive officer of the corporation. The agent, who resided in Manchester, served as the chief operating officer in charge of the mills. The president served as a relatively inactive chairman of the board of directors. Amory, who has previously held the position of treasurer of the Jackson Manufacturing Co. of Nashua, N.H., became Amoskeag's treasurer and agent in 1837. A separate agent was appointed in 1841 but Mr. Amory served as treasurer until he was appointed president in 1877, a position he held until his death in 1888. Amory was instrumental in the decision to expand production to the east side of the river.

Ezekiel Straw, who began his employment with Amoskeag as an engineer in 1838, went on to become the first of three generations of his family to serve as Amoskeag's agent. Straw later served as governor of the state from 1872 to 1873. The minutes of the Board of Directors of the Amoskeag show that during his tenure as Governor he received a quarterly stipend of $1,000 to supplement his state salary. The fact that this was recorded in the minutes would lead one to assume that the practice was considered appropriate and completely above board.

The history of Amoskeag in the nineteenth century is really a history of five separate corporations that shared common stockholders and overlapping management. All of these corporations were ultimately merged together in the next century. Amoskeag was by far the largest of the five. In addition to manufacturing cotton textiles, Amoskeag also constructed and operated the canal system, built its own mills and the mills of its sister corporations, and maintained an extensive machine shop and foundry for the production of textile machinery that it sold throughout New England. The other four corporations were Stark, which specialized in the manufacture of duck cloth; Merrimack, later named Manchester Print Works, which produced woolen cloth; and Langdon and Amory, which both produced cotton material.

The general practice of the "Boston Associates," a name given to the various groups of Massachusetts investors who organized the development of the various textile communities throughout New England, was to form new corporations when they planned a substantial capacity increase or when they moved into the production of a different type of cloth. Usually the new corporations had many of the same stockholders as the older corporations in the same community.

The first mill constructed on the east side of the river was for the Stark Manufacturing Company, incorporated in 1838. Stark and Amoskeag shared similar stockholders and a common management with William Amory serving as the treasurer of both corporations. The original mill was completed in 1839. That same year a second mill north of the original mill was started and completed. Five years later Amoskeag built a connecting structure 100 feet long, at which time the total complex became known as Stark No. 1. Shortly after the completion of the first section of the Stark, Amoskeag's new upper canal was completed and in June 24, 1939, the canal was filled and started providing Stark with water power leased from Amoskeag.

The same year that the Stark was organized, the Manchester Mills was chartered. Like the Stark, it has similar shareholders as Amoskeag. While it purchased a mill site from Amoskeag at that time, it did not have a mill constructed until six years later. This company went on to specialize in the manufacture and printing of delaines, a thin woolen material with a printed pattern.

In 1840, Amoskeag saw the opportunity for the successful expansion of manufacturing capacity in Manchester. Amoskeag's original intention at that time was to form a new corporation to own and manage this endeavor. However, the investors were not receptive to this opportunity and thus Amoskeag constructed the mill for its own use. This represented its first mill owned and operated by Amoskeag on the east side of the river.

During the remainder of the nineteenth century, Amoskeag used two methods for expansion of mills in Manchester. On some occasions it would construct mills for its own use. On other instances it would build for Stark or Manchester or a new corporation with overlapping management and ownership.

In addition to building mills, Amoskeag also built housing for the workers. Since Amoskeag followed the "Lowell System" of recruiting young women from rural farm families to tend the looms in the mills, the original mill residences were boarding houses. The corporation imposed strict rules for the residents. There was a ten o'clock curfew. Alcoholic consumption was prohibited. Weekly church attendance was mandatory. While these regulations seem prohibitive by today's standards, they provided a sense of security to the Yankee rural families that were considering sending their daughters to Manchester to work in the mills.

In later years, when immigrant families replaced the "mill girls" as the primary source of workers, these boarding houses were converted into tenements suitable for family residence. Even after the conversion to tenements, the corporation maintained a paternalistic outlook with conditions of employment stating, "The company will not employ any one who is habitually absent from public worship on the Sabbath, or who uses profane or indecent language in the mills or elsewhere, or who uses ardent spirits as a beverage." This condition of employment was still used as late as 1873.

On October 24, 1838, Amoskeag held the first of four public auctions of land for individuals desiring to construct commercial and residential buildings. In all, 57 lots were sold. The following October a second public offering was made for land located south of the original offering. These lots sold at a substantial premium over the original lots, reflecting the growth in population and prosperity that the Stark mill had brought to the new town.

From its origin as a corporation in 1835, Amoskeag was a responsible corporate citizen, realizing that the promotion of adequate facilities for its workers and the community would have long-run benefits to the company. For this reason it either donated or sold at half price land for various schools that the city decided to build. At the same time the corporation was holding its land auctions, it set aside parcels for parks. Between 1848 and 1852 these parcels were donated to the city at no cost. In a similar manner Amoskeag deeded to the city free of charge almost 20 acres to be used as the cemetery.

In 1840, the Corporation donated a lot to the First Baptist Church, which had decided to move from its original location in Amoskeag Village to the east side of the river. Like many of Amoskeag's bequests, this was of mutual benefit to both the recipient and the donor. The church would benefit from the savings on land costs while locating on the side of the river to which its parishioners were gravitating. Amoskeag would benefit inasmuch as its workers were ensured of a place of worship near corporate housing.

When the "Manchester Athenaeum," the forerunner of the city library, was formed in 1844 by a group of Manchester citizens, it received the support of Amoskeag and its auxiliary mills. In 1846, Amoskeag donated $1,000 while Stark donated another $500. The following year the Manchester Print Works donated an additional $500. In 1871, when the city, which had taken over the athenaeum, decided to construct a new library building, Amoskeag donated a building lot.

Amoskeag gained worldwide recognition for the production of its machine shop and foundry that were first opened in 1840. In addition to producing textile equipment for its own and other mills, it also produced railroad locomotives and fire engines. Between 1849 and 1859, 232 steam locomotives were produced for major railroads in the United States. In 1859, this business was sold to the Manchester Locomotive Works and the shop turned to the production of steam

FIRST BAPTIST CHURCH

UPPER YARD

fire engines. The company produced 550 such fire engines. In 1877, this business was also sold to the Manchester Locomotive Works. During the Civil War, Amoskeag contracted to produce over 25,000 muskets for the government.

In 1860, the Langdon Manufacturing Corporation, which had been chartered some three years earlier, held an organizational meeting. Like the Stark and Manchester Mills it shared stockholders and directors with Amoskeag. Gardner Brewer, Amoskeag's selling agent, and William Amory, Amoskeag's treasurer, were among the original directors. By 1868, the capital stock had been increased to $500,000.

In 1865, Amoskeag expanded the variety of its textile line to include ginghams, a yarn-dyed plain weaved cotton fabric that became the company's primary product for many years. To facilitate this move into the new product, the company solicited skilled weavers from both England and Scotland. These prospective workers were required to show references involving the quality of their work, their general character and their church attendance prior to being hired by Amoskeag. In addition to recruiting these female weavers, Amoskeag also acquired the services of men from Scotland and Germany to assist in the management of the gingham weaving and dyeing processes.

In the 1870's, the Manchester Mill, which had been a successful operation in its earlier years, was experiencing declining prosperity. In 1874, the mills were sold to outside interests that formed a new corporation. Following this reorganization there was no longer an overlapping directorship with Amoskeag. The Manchester Mill operated as a separate corporation until early into the next century.

In 1879, the Amory Manufacturing Co., named after William Amory, its first president, was organized. A letter was sent to all Amoskeag stockholders inviting them to subscribe to stock of the new corporation. The letter on the next page demonstrates the relationship between Amoskeag and its associated corporations.

In 1887, a merger of Amory and Langdon was completed when

Boston

November 1, 1879

To the Stockholders of the
Amoskeag Manufacturing Co.

Gentlemen:

A charter has been granted to the Amory Manufacturing Co. by the State of New Hampshire.

The City of Manchester, having agreed to a remission of taxes for ten years, work was begun in the construction of a mill of 50,000 spindles.

This mill will be completed and running during the year 1880. The contract for building and for machinery are very favorable and the Amoskeag Manufacturing Co. has agreed to convey to the new company the real estate which it occupies free of charge, besides sufficient real estate on the opposite side of the river for boarding houses if it requires them. Under these circumstances it is probable that the new corporation will be able to manufacture profitably.

The capital for the Amory Manufacturing Co. will be $900,000 = divided into 9,000 shares of one hundred dollars each. This will give about $200,000 = quick capital.

Every stockholder of the Amoskeag Manufacturing Co. of record December 1, 1879 will have the privilege of subscribing to two shares of the Amory Manufacturing Co. at par for each share that he then owns in the Amoskeag Manufacturing Co.

Payments to be made of twenty-five dollars a share December 15, 1879, February 16, April 15 and June 15, 1880. Any stockholder who does not make the first payment on December 15, 1879 will be considered to have waived his right to subscribe for the new stock and the Directors of the Amory Manufacturing Co. will distribute any shares not taken December 15, 1879 to the public, at private or public sale provided no share be sold below par.

Five percent interest will be allowed on pre-payment of the subscriptions.

To the directors of the Amoskeag Manufacturing Co. on being notified by the Treasurer of the Amory Manufacturing Co. that 6,000 shares of the new stock have been subscribed for and are fully paid will pay over $300,000 = to the Amory Manufacturing Co. for the 3,000 = shares still left and will distribute them share for share among the stockholders of the Amoskeag Manufacturing Co. of record December 1, 1879.

By order of the Directors
    T. Jefferson Coolidge, Treasurer
    Amoskeag Manufacturing Co.

each share of Langdon, with a par value of $1,000 was exchanged for nine shares on Amory, each with a par value of $100. This merger brought the number of separate corporations producing textiles in Manchester down from five to four.

Following the retirement of William Amory in 1876, the role of treasurer was taken over by T. Jefferson Coolidge. Coolidge, like Amory, was of Boston aristocracy. His service as treasurer, which was in three different terms, ended in 1896. The first interruption was in the four years beginning in 1880 when he served as president of the Atcheson, Topeka & Santa Fe Railroad which was experiencing financial difficulty at that time. Mr. Coolidge's second leave from the treasurership was in the years 1892 and 1893 when he served as Minister to France. Following Coolidge's retirement in 1896, the treasurership was taken over by Charles W. Amory, the second son of William Amory. The younger Amory remained in that role until 1905.

Following E. A. Straw's retirement in 1879, the position of agent was first held by Thomas L. Livermore. In 1885 the position was taken over by Herman F. Straw, the second of three generations of Straws who held the position. Herman Straw, who first became employed by Amoskeag in 1872 when his father was still agent, served as the primary operating manager of the firm from his appointment as agent in 1885 until his retirement in 1920.

While Amoskeag and its sister corporations experienced near constant expansion through the nineteenth century, one new plant construction deserves particular attention. In 1886, Amoskeag's No. 10 or Jefferson Mill was constructed. The significance of this construction was that it was motorized by steam power, since the prior mill expansion had exhausted the hydro power provided by the Merrimack River. By this time many other New England textile manufacturers had embarked on a policy of expansion in the South where the lower wage rate created the opportunity for greater profits. At the time of the Jefferson Mill construction many — in and out of the industry — praised Amoskeag for its devotion to the city.

One final significant event in the history of Manchester's textile mills prior to the emergence of F. C. Dumaine as the dominant force in the city's manufacturing was the sale of the Stark Mills. In 1901, the Stark Corporation was absorbed into the U.S. Cotton Duck Corporation when the stockholders accepted a cash offer of $1,500 per share. Prior to the merger, the book value of Stark was $1,800 per share while the market price per share was $975. The fact that Stark was selling at approximately 50 percent of its book value is indicative of the competition found in the duck cloth market at that time. U. S. Cotton Duck had been formed the prior year through the merger of mills in Maryland and Connecticut in the North, and South Carolina, Alabama and Georgia in the South. This was one of the first attempts to form a trust in a section of the textile industry. The goal of the 1900 merger was to form a cartel in the manufacturing of heavy duck cloth. The rationale behind the move was similar to most trust formations at the time, that is to gain some market power in an extremely competitive industry. However, like many of the industries in which entry was possible, the raising of prices by the trust firms led other firms in peripheral industries to alter their products to fill the demand of the market left by the monopoly pricing. Stark specialized in the manufacturer of lightweight duck cloth. It was a relatively simple procedure to alter their manufacturing process to produce a heavier weight cloth. This was the primary reason that U. S. Cotton Duck was willing to pay such a substantial premium over the market price to gain control of the Stark mills. In retrospect, U.S. Cotton Duck gained little market dominance from either the 1900 or the 1901 merger because of subsequent entry of new firms into the heavy duck cotton market.

The competitiveness of the textile market in general is an important point for the reader to remember. While competition resulted in better prices for the general public, it also meant that for a firm to survive, and thus be able to continue to provide employment to its workers, its costs must be in line with the most efficient in the industry. As more and more textile mills were constructed in the low labor cost areas in the South, the severity of this problem for Northern mills increased.

Prior to this sale to U. S. Cotton Duck, Stark continued to share a close working relationship with Amoskeag. Throughout most of these years, both corporations employed the same selling agents. William Amory of Amoskeag served as Stark's treasurer from its inception

The Stark Mills

through 1876 except for a period of time in 1848 to 1852 when his son Charles Amory was the treasurer. At the time of the sale, Sidney Coolidge, brother of T. Jefferson Coolidge, was Stark's treasurer. He remained in this position following the acquisition until 1903 when the office of treasurer was abolished and the mills' books were transferred to corporate headquarters. At this point, U. S. Cotton Duck gradually shifted production of many of Stark's more profitable lines to its lower labor cost plants in the South, while continuing to market the products under Stark's brand names. This separation of management continued until 1922, when Amoskeag acquired the Stark Mills from International Cotton Mills, which then owned the property of U. S. Cotton Duck. International had decided to permanently halt production in the Manchester plants and move all of its production to its Southern locations.

Before embarking on a study of F.C. Dumaine's stewardship of Amoskeag, it is useful to summarize the state of textile manufacturing as Manchester entered into the twentieth century. In 1901, there were four principal manufacturers in the city. Amoskeag Manufacturing Company employed about 8,000 workers in plants that were constantly kept up to date. Amory Manufacturing Company, which included the merged Langdon Mills, employed 1,400 workers and shared a common management with Amoskeag. Like Amoskeag, it set aside sufficient profits to ensure that machinery and plant were in proper order. Stark Mills employed about 1,600 workers. However, the recent sale of its assets to U. S. Cotton Duck severed any overlapping directorships with Amoskeag or Amory. The Manchester Mills, which formerly had employed up to 3,000 workers, had not shared a common management with Amoskeag since its reorganization in 1874. The last quarter of the nineteenth century was not good to the Manchester Mill. Employment was down and the lack of adequate profits prevented management from making sufficient reinvestment necessary to keep the plant in a state-of-the-art condition.

Contrary to the policies of many Northern based manufacturers of diversifying production to the South, Amoskeag appeared dedicated to expansion through the construction of new plants in Manchester. Amoskeag built the Jefferson Mill in 1886 and Mill No. 11 in 1889 despite the threat of increased capacity by Southern mills with lower labor costs. The fact that these mills were coal driven accentuates the dedication of Amoskeag directors to the citizens of Manchester. The Merrimack River could no longer provide new plants with an energy cost advantage to help offset the South's labor cost advantage. The competitive response experienced by the U. S. Cotton Duck Trust illustrated the need to keep overall costs in line if Amoskeag and its sister corporations hoped to continue to provide employment to the workers of Manchester. This was the challenge facing Amoskeag's next treasurer.

F. C. DUMAINE

Chapter III

Restructuring Amoskeag Under Dumaine

Unlike his predecessors as treasurer of Amoskeag, Dumaine was not from Boston aristocracy. He was born on March 6, 1866, in Hadley, Massachusetts, into a family of modest means. Dumaine's father, Christopher, had emigrated from Quebec with his wife Cordelia and his three stepdaughters. Christopher moved his family to Dedham in 1886 when he obtained a position as a foreman in the broom factory of David A. Baker. While not rich, the family was comfortable on Christopher's wages. By 1874, when the two oldest stepdaughters, Elizabeth and Relena, were married, Christopher could afford to send the third daughter, Georgia, to a preparatory school at Antioch College in Ohio.

During his tenure in Dedham, Christopher was active as a volunteer fireman with Engine Company Hero Number One. On the evening of January 7, 1878, in subzero temperature, the company responded to a fire. After fighting the fire through most of the night, Christopher contracted pneumonia. Since there were no antibiotics to fight off infections, the general practice was to administer alcohol to the patient. The consensus among doctors at that time was that if one survived to the ninth day the fever would break and the patient would live. Young Fred, who assisted his mother, Cordelia, in nursing Christopher never forgot his father struggling to breathe, propped up with pillows in a big armchair. On the eighth day Christopher died.

To add to young Dumaine's pain of the loss of his father, that spring his stepsister Georgia suffered a crippling fall that would leave her disabled all her life.

To help with his family's support, Fred began working in Henry Pettingall's local dry goods store. After a year, he felt he deserved a raise that he didn't get so he left and subsequently worked for a screen man and then in McLaughlin's shoe store.

In 1880, T. Jefferson Coolidge was looking for an office boy and Dumaine came to his attention. Fred borrowed $16 to buy a three-month commuter ticket from Dedham to Boston so he could work in Coolidge's Boston office for $4 a week.

Dumaine's diligence impressed Coolidge and office manager Lucius M. Sargent, and Dumaine idolized both as father figures. He later would attribute his success to the apprenticeship he served there.

His diligence was rewarded with increased responsibility, leading him to be promoted to an assistant in the purchasing department. In 1888, he moved to board in Boston with the intention of attending night school. All the while, he continued his practice of sending half his paycheck back to Dedham to help with the support of his mother and stepsister.

Eventually, Dumaine was sent to Manchester to work in the Jefferson Mill to learn the manufacturing side of the business. The only records of Dumaine's residency in Manchester appears in the 1891 and 1892 city directories. The 1891 edition had the following listing:

Dumaine Fred C. rooms 44 Walnut

The standard format in the directory was to list the names of all adult males and widows and single adult females. Following the name was the individual's occupation and/or location of employment, type of residence (house, boards or rooms) and the location of the residence. Unmarried adults residing in the family home were listed as boarding.

The fact that there was no listing of Amoskeag as Dumaine's employer probably reflects that the census taker did not obtain that information. The listing of "rooms" indicates that young Dumaine, then 25 years old, was renting a room without the meals that would have accompanied the term "boards."

The 1892 edition of the Manchester Directory had the following listing:

YOUNG FRED (RIGHT) WORKING IN THE AMOSKEAG MILLS IN MANCHESTER, ABOUT 1891

Dumaine Fred C. removed to Boston, Mass.

The term "removed" was used to signify that the person had relocated to the designated city.

Apparently Dumaine found his exposure to Manchester and the manufacturing process beneficial because a generation later he would send F.C. Dumaine, Jr., his eldest son and ultimate successor as treasurer of Amoskeag, to attain a similar education in Manchester.

Dumaine had been called back to replace the purchasing manager who had died. With his return to Boston he was given more and more responsibilities. Two years later he was transferred to selling and accounting.

In the meantime, he met and, in 1895, he married Bessie Thomas, a direct descendent of Isaiah Thomas, the printer, publisher and patriot of Revolutionary War fame. In 1904, when he began keeping a diary, a practice he picked up from T. Jefferson Coolidge, his first entry was:

> On the 13th of April, 1895, I married Elizabeth Thomas. This was the turning point of my life. It brought me the happiness of a home life, gave me the companionship of a true woman, which filled me with responsibility and ambitions; and from that time I commenced to know life as it is. My future success, if there be any for me, dates from that event.

At age eighteen Elizabeth Thomas was eleven years younger than F.C. They were to have seven children born between the years 1897 and 1912. Following the birth of their youngest child, Bessie became active in the Woman's Suffrage Movement. On May 2, 1914, against F.C.'s wishes, she carried the American flag as the suffragists marched up Beacon Hill in Boston.

The couple separated in 1916. Whether the cause was the age difference, F.C.'s work load which kept him preoccupied with business matters, or Dumaine's French Canadian heritage which caused him to expect her to remain in the home is unknown. The separation ended in a divorce in 1919. Following the separation and subsequent divorce, the four oldest children remained with F.C., while the three youngest lived with their mother.

In 1898, Dumaine was appointed treasurer of the Amory Manufacturing Co. Three years later he was elected an Amory director. Dumaine's first major task as a treasurer was with the Manchester Mill during its reorganization. As mentioned earlier, this corporation was managed by a different group of investors with no overlap in directorships since 1874. Since its separation from Amoskeag, this corporation, with a capitalized investment of $2,000,000, met with mixed success. While it did succeed in paying dividends over most of those years, by 1903 it had need of substantial additional capital for purchasing new equipment. The directors of Manchester Mills approved the issue of $2,000,000 new preferred stock to which the existing common stockholders could subscribe on a prorated basis. Very little interest was shown on the part of these shareholders. T. Jefferson Coolidge, Amoskeag's current president, offered to subscribe to all the new securities in his own behalf under the following conditions. The current shareholders must reduce their original $2,000,000 to $500,000 and sell their common shares to Coolidge at this reduced value. This offer was accepted by the Manchester Mill's shareholders. The net effect was that Amoskeag interests acquired the entire mill and print works for $500,000 and planned to invest an additional $2,000,000 for equipment and working capital.

On the same day the stockholders accepted Coolidge's offer, the board of directors was replaced with an Amoskeag board. F.C. Dumaine, who was an employee in the Amoskeag Treasurer's office and the current treasurer at the Amory, was appointed treasurer of the newly organized Manchester Mills. Again it should be pointed out that the treasurer in New England textile manufacturers functioned as the chief executive officer for the corporation. During the next 30 months over half of the $2 million generated by the preferred stock issue was spent on new equipment. In his October 1905 report to the Directors of the Manchester Mills, Dumaine stated:

> The managers directly in charge of the operations at the mill feel
> confident the concern is now thoroughly first class and up to date
> in every important detail. Many economies have been inaugu-
> rated, departments concentrated, and all possible savings in run-
> ning expenses made.

In 1905, Dumaine succeeded Charles W. Amory as Amoskeag's

treasurer. This was the first time that the position was held by an individual that would not have been characterized as a "proper Bostonian." Dumaine came from a socioeconomic background more like the employees that he would eventually manage than that of prior Amoskeag treasurers.

In the same year, the directors of Amoskeag decided to merge the Amoskeag, the Manchester Mills and the Amory, the three companies under their control at that time. While the merger called for a cash purchase of the shares of the Amory and Manchester companies, the shareholders were allowed the option to invest the majority of their proceeds in new shares of Amoskeag, the acquiring company. To facilitate the stock exchange, Amoskeag had a ten for one stock split. Just prior to the merger the 1,000 shares of $1,000 par value was changed to 10,000 shares of $100 par value. Following the exercise of the stock options on the part of the former Amory and Manchester stockholders, the Amoskeag's outstanding capital was increased to $5.76 million.

AMOSKEAG PRODUCTION AND SALES 1906 - 1911

In Millions of Yards

Year	Amoskeag Dept. *Cotton Cloth*	Manchester *Worsted Cloth*	Total Cloth *Cotton & Worsted*
1906-1907			
Production	172.5	14.9	187.4
Sales	169.8	15.0	184.8
1907-1908			
Production	159.9	12.3	172.2
Sales	149.1	11.9	161.0
1908-1909			
Production	171.4	13.9	185.4
Sales	180.8	13.8	194.6
1909-1910			
Production	191.9	16.2	208.0
Sales	185.1	16.5	201.6
1910-1911			
Production	205.2	14.2	219.4
Sales	207.5	14.5	222.0
Total 5 Years			
Production	901.0	71.4	972.5
Sales	892.3	71.7	964.3

The previous chart summarizes the production of cloth for the five years following the merger.

The five-year income account for the period from July 1906 to May 1911 is given below. For the reader unfamiliar with accounting procedures during this period, it is important to note that Amoskeag was on a "pure" cash basis relative to investments. Therefore, the five income statement items shown can be interpreted as almost equivalent to actual cash flows. If Amoskeag were to invest a portion of its revenue in new machinery, this would be treated as an expense as opposed to being capitalized and subsequently depreciated over the equipment's useful life. In terms of today's accounting standards, this practice had the impact of underestimating actual profit margins in years where substantial capital investments were made and of overstating the profits in subsequent years when depreciation was not recognized. The sales represent the dollar revenue received by the firm. The expenses or costs represent the cash paid for labor, materials, overhead and new capital equipment. There would be no depreciation expense, since equipment was not capitalized. The net profits are the differences between the sales, or cash revenue, and the expenses, which included cash disbursements for operations and also investments in new plants and equipment. The dividends are that portion of the profits that were paid out to the stockholders, with the surplus representing the remaining portion of the profits that were kept in the business.

AMOSKEAG INCOME ACCOUNT 1906-1911

In $1,000s

	1906-07	1907-08	1908-09	1909-10	1910-11
Sales	$17,880	$16,109	$16,967	$20,477	$21,559
Expenses	16,648	14,858	16,185	19,716	20,837
Net Profit	$ 1,232	$ 1,251	$ 782	$ 761	$ 22
Dividends	922	922	691	691	691
Surplus	$ 310	$ 329	$ 91	$ 70	$ 31

The balance sheets for the five-year period are presented on the next page. In reference to the assets, it is important to know that the company's conservative accounting practice called for evaluating the plant at $3 million, while the actual value would be about four times that price. The net effect of this conservative practice was that the book value of the equity was underestimated by some $9 million. While the items listed as assets are similar to those used in accounting today, the various liabilities are significantly different and merit explanation. The capital represents the investments in the business when the corporation sells stock. The bills payable represent short-term trade credit. The corporation had no long-term debt. The reserve for depreciation, profit and loss and surplus added together would be equivalent to retained earnings in today's accounting practices. The net quick would be equivalent to new working capital, that is, current assets less current liabilities. In the balance sheet, net quick represents inventory plus cash and accounts receivable less bills payable.

Amoskeag's conservative accounting practice of expensing the construction of new plants prevents the reader from seeing the impact of the corporation's expansion effect on its balance sheet. In 1909, Amoskeag had two significant investments. The significance was both in the size and the implication of the investments. In that year, the company built the $2 million Coolidge Mill on the west side of the river. The plant was expected to require over 2,000 additional workers, bringing the total labor force to about 15,000. In addition, Amoskeag constructed a new coal power house to generate electricity for the expanded capacity. The implication of the construction of a mill on the west side of the river was that there were no canals and therefore no water power. The requirement to build a power plant further emphasized this fact. Amoskeag had exhausted the cheap energy source of the Merrimack River. The corporation knew that if the mill had been constructed in the South, they would have had labor costs some 40 percent lower. The directors and Treasurer Dumaine were continuing the practice of expanding capacity in Manchester.

In May of 1911, the organization of Amoskeag was changed from a corporation to a trust. The significance of this legal alteration was that the twelve trustees, composed of the eight former directors and four new members, had greater latitude in the management of the corporation. At the same time that the organizational form of the

BALANCE SHEETS
In $1,000s

	1906	1907	1908	1909	1910
			Assets		
Mills & Mach'y	$ 3,000	$ 3,000	$ 3,000	$ 3,000	$ 3,000
Inventory	4,348	964	786	3,913	3,030
Cash and Acct. Rec.	4,506	7,305	6,164	5,281	7,461
Totals	$11,854	$11,269	$ 9,950	$12,194	$13,491
			Claims		
Capital	$ 5,760	$ 5,760	$ 5,760	$ 5,760	$ 5,760
Bills Pay.	2,175	1,075	50	1,300	2,655
Res. Dep.	500	500			
Prof. & Loss	1,451	1,913	1,579	1,671	1,740
Surplus	1,968	2,022	2,561	3,463	3,336
Totals	$11,854	$11,269	$ 9,950	$12,194	$13,491
Net Quick	$ 4,919	$ 7,194	$ 6,900	$ 7,894	$ 7,836
Book Value Par Share	$116	$125	$120	$137	$135

business was changed, Amoskeag's capital stock was increased through a five-for-one stock split. Each of the 57,600 shares of $100 par value common stock was replaced with three shares of no par common that began paying $3 annual dividend each and two shares of 4.5 percent $100 par preferred. The net effect of this change was that a former shareholder, who had been receiving $12 on an old share, now was receiving a total of $18 on the five new shares.

The significance of the increase in dividends associated with the stock split was that the trustees felt the prosperity experienced during this period could be expected to continue and that they would be able to maintain the dividend pay out in future years without dipping into the surplus. The act of exchanging one $100 par value share (with a market price in the range of $300) for three shares of common stock and two shares of preferred stock was probably to facilitate trading for investors wishing to purchase or liquidate their Amoskeag holdings. It is certain that the book value per share of approximately $140 underestimated the true worth of the old stock. This understatement was primarily a result of expensing capital investments, such as the Coolidge Mill. However, since Amoskeag did not write up its assets at the time of changing the corporate form to a trust, a practice that was prevalent at the time, the trustees elected to issue the new stock on a no par basis.

The fact that the organization was transferred from a corporation to a trust should not lead the reader to assume that this meant that Amoskeag was in the process of establishing monopoly power. While it was the world's largest cotton textile firm, its market share never exceeded 4 percent. It is true that its share of the gingham market was significantly higher: however, if one reflects on the U. S. Cotton Duck-Stark situation discussed earlier, the fallacy of assuming that the market should be defined in narrow product lines becomes apparent. While Amoskeag had a quality reputation, it did not dominate the market. The true significance of the trust formation as used here is that it empowered the trustees, formerly the directors, with greater discretion in the management of the corporation.

It is interesting to note that the unpublished history devoted little attention to the growth in Southern textile firms during this period of time. When Amoskeag constructed the Coolidge Mill and the power plant in 1909, the company was aware of the possibility of constructing alternative facilities in the South, thereby taking advantage of the lower labor costs.

Obviously Amoskeag was continuing its corporate social policy of looking out for their current employee. But, the directors were practical businessmen. In addition to having a desirable goal, that of maintaining employment in Manchester, they must have felt that it could be accomplished. For this to be successful in the long run they needed equal labor costs.

One rationale could have been to assume that the superior skills of New England mill workers would allow Amoskeag to compete at the wage rate differential. To this day, critics of Dumaine cite this as a reason why the wage rate difference was not a sufficient cause to close Amoskeag. It seems unlikely that Amoskeag's management would have fallen a victim of this error. Dumaine had already seen Amoskeag's workforce shift from imported Scottish weavers and Yankee farm girls to include immigrant Irish, Franco-Canadian, Polish and Greek workers. Each ethnic group successfully integrated into the mill setting as a response to the economic incentives.

It is more likely that Amoskeag's directors expected that the white workers employed in Southern mills and the black workers that would soon follow them would respond to the same economic incentives and soon reach the quality and quantity equivalent of a New England mill worker.

A second rationale for believing that Amoskeag could be successful in this corporate social policy would be to assume that the superior administrative skills in Boston combined with the potential for increased organizational costs operating over a wider geographical area made the move to the South seem risky. This also appears unlikely. Improvements in transportation and communication now made the effective distance from Boston to the South much less then when Amoskeag was first organized in Manchester.

A more probable explanation for Amoskeag's optimism for its long-term competitive ability, was that to presume that labor market forces in the South would result in wage pressures that over a relatively short time would bring about near wage equality.

Regardless of the basis for the optimism, Amoskeag built the Coolidge mill and the new power plant. Critics of the free market system applauded this as an instance in which the conscience of the corporation caused it to make a socially beneficial investment earning "satisfactory profits" rather then pushing for maximum profits. At the time, many praised Amoskeag's balanced outlook. With the advantage of hindsight, we might today question whether this was truly in society's best long-term interest. The future expansion of mill construction in the South would ultimately cause the market price of textiles to drop to a point where Amoskeag's "satisfactory profits" turned into "unsatisfactory losses," a situation that would not have occurred had the firm acquiesced to the greed of profit maximization.

It was one option for Amoskeag to acquire existing Amory and Manchester plants with an eye on maintaining the current employment levels. Since the corporations had similar owners, it was virtually an exchange of the stock of one corporation for the stock of another corporation which many of the shareholders already owned. In fact, the merger resulted in a partial liquidation dividend because the sellers of Amory and Manchester stock were not allowed to exchange all of their stock for Amoskeag stock but received a portion in cash.

It was an altogether different proposition to embark on new plant construction the size of Coolidge, increasing employment and production in a section of the country having a significant cost disadvantage. Had the mill been constructed in the South, it would have provided the same number of new jobs. In fact, it could be argued that the lower wage rate there reflected a greater need for jobs in that section of the country. The advantage of the Southern location was that the jobs created would not have been destined to a premature death due to increasing competition from lower cost producers.

Old Manchester Mill

No. 11 Mill

Chapter IV

The Expansion of Production and Employee Benefits

In the five years following the May 1911 change to a trust organization, Amoskeag experienced its greatest physical production and employment. Through the merger with Amory and Manchester and the construction of the Coolidge, Amoskeag had become the world's largest textile manufacturer. It was also over this period that Amoskeag substantially increased the benefit programs available for its employees. This chapter will begin with a review of the financial progress made by the firm in this five-year period and will end with a summary of the advances made by the employees over the same time period.

The table below records the production and sales during this period.

Amoskeag Production & Sales

Cloth in millions of yards. Bags in thousands of units.

Cloth & Bags Produced

Year	Cotton	Worsteds	Total Cloth	Bags
1911-12	223.8	12.3	236.3	637.3
1912-13	217.5	14.1	231.6	823.5
1913-14	221.3	13.7	235.0	1,179.3
1914-15	200.4	13.5	214.1	1,491.0
1915-16	188.3	12.3	200.6	1,713.3
Totals	1,051.4	65.9	1,117.6	5,844.5

Cloth & Bags Sold

Year	Cotton & Worsted Cloth	Bags
1911-12	236.0	833.0
1912-13	231.7	864.9
1913-14	229.6	1,169.4
1914-15	217.7	1,487.4
1915-16	201.6	1,715.8
Totals	1,116.6	6,070.5

While the five-year period represented the greatest level of output, both the production and sales figures demonstrate declines from the 1911-12 highs. The exception was in bag production, which showed an increase as the result of the construction of a new bag mill in 1914. This decline, which was to continue for the remainder of Amoskeag's history, was a result of increased competition from continually expanding production by the South. This had a nominal impact on both the revenue and the profit margins as shown by the income statements for the same five years. The profit margin did recover temporarily beginning in 1914-15 as a result of increased prices associated with the war situation in Europe.

AMOSKEAG INCOME ACCOUNT
$1,000's

	1911-12	1912-13	1913-14	1914-15	1915-16
Sales	$20,767	$21,517	$20,658	$19,125	$20,684
Expenses	19,663	20,455	19,634	18,046	19,505
Net Income	$ 1,104	$ 1,062	$ 1,024	$ 1,079	$ 1,179
Dividends	1,035	1,037	1,037	1,037	1,037
Surplus	$ 69	$ 26	($ 13)	$ 43	$ 142
Income/Sales	5.3%	4.9%	4.9%	5.6%	5.7%
Earnings per Common Share	$ 3.59	$ 3.21	$ 2.92	$ 3.25	$ 3.82

On January 1, 1914, the 55-hour workweek was legalized, replacing the previous 58-hour week. Amoskeag decided to maintain the same weekly wage, granting, in effect, a 5.5 percent hourly increase. The following statement was printed in the company paper:

> At this time of nationwide industrial depression and uncertainty, when securities of all kinds have shrunk to the lowest level seen for years, with the strong possibility that the end is not yet, when the great industries that give people employment see themselves

confronted with a lack of orders and the consequent deplorable necessity of a reduction in their working forces, the action of the Amoskeag Manufacturing Company in keeping the 55-hour weekly wage the same as the 58-hour weekly wage stands out with special significance.

In the face of a very unsettled gingham and dress goods market, brought about by the reduction in tariff rates by the present administration, reasons were at hand in abundance to keep the hourly rate the same. It means that $350 thousand and $400 thousand more money will be paid to Amoskeag employees each year than would have been paid, and this amount must be lost by the shareholders.

Toward the end of 1914, Amoskeag began to experience increased sales as a result of war orders. Two products that experienced increased demand were barracks bags and worsted cloth (used for the production of military uniforms). The company granted two five percent wage increases in 1916, a reflection of increased demand for labor and inflation associated with military production.

Amoskeag's balance sheets in this five-year period are shown on the next page. This is a more condensed version than the balance sheet presented in the previous chapter. In this format, all cash, receivables and inventories, have been condensed into one line titled assets. On the liability side, all equity accounts, capital, profit and loss and surplus, are combined in the reserves and profit and loss line. The most significant factor illustrated by the balance sheet is that the company's net working capital continued to grow despite paying the higher dividends established in the 1911 restructuring.

As the statements demonstrate, Amoskeag continued to show the value of plants at the nominal $3 million level. By 1916, the City of Manchester had assessed the property at $17.5 million. While many criticized this conservative approach as being misleading, Dumaine felt that it was better to err toward conservatism then to value plants at cost, less accumulated depreciation, without regard to fluctuations in current market values.

From its incorporation in 1831, Amoskeag tried to provide its

Amoskeag Balance Sheet (Oct. 1, 1911-1916)

In $1,000's

	1912	1913	1914	1915	1916
		Assets			
Real Estate & Machinery	$ 3,000	$ 3,000	$ 3,000	$ 3,000	$ 3,000
Current Assets	10,787	10,617	10,644	10,594	14,876
Totals	$ 13,787	$ 13,617	$ 13,644	$ 13,594	$ 17,876
		Claims			
Accounts Payable	$ 1,426	$ 1,093	$ 1,129	$ 886	$ 4,841
Equity	12,361	12,524	12,535	12,709	13,035
Totals	$ 13,787	$ 13,617	$ 13,644	$ 13,594	$ 17,876
Net Working Capital	$ 9,361	$ 9,523	$ 9,515	$ 9,709	$ 10,036

workers with pleasant working and living conditions. As mentioned in Chapter II, the company built boarding houses for its workers when they were drawing primarily "mill girls" from the surrounding farms. When the growth in work force came by way of immigration from Europe and Franco Canada, these boarding houses were converted to tenements and additional tenements were constructed. For many second generation citizens of Manchester, employment at the Amoskeag would begin on a part-time basis while in school. As the children would terminate their schooling, often at an early age, they would seek permanent employment in the mills. While Amoskeag continued to be Manchester's most important industrial employer in the early twentieth century, it was experiencing increasing competition for the labor force from new industries within the city and throughout New England.

At the same time, Amoskeag was seeking alternative measures to reduce its manufacturing costs to offset the decline in its profit margin. To a great extent, this lower profit margin was the result of lower prices caused by increased production by Southern mills. In order for Amoskeag to be competitive in such an environment, its markup over manufacturing costs on the cloth had to be lowered. This phenomena would continue to reduce Amoskeag's profit margin as long as Southern firms could expect to earn a reasonable profit on their increased capacity. The company formed a time-study unit and a centralized employment office.

Dumaine felt that if Amoskeag were to continue to retain the employment without putting additional pressure on wage rates, which had to be kept to a minimum, then the company needed to expand its corporate welfare system. The responsibility for the initiation and carrying out of this program was left to W. Parker Straw, the third of three generations of Straws to eventually serve as the company agent, who held the position of superintendent at this time.

In 1910, the Textile Club was organized to provide additional recreational, educational and social activities for the employees. The organization's goals were expressed in the articles of incorporation:

> To advance the acquaintanceship of the employees of the Amoskeag Manufacturing Company with each other; to provide athletics and healthy sports; to purchase, lease and otherwise acquire, deal in, and otherwise dispose of, any and all real and personal estate and other property and things whatsoever deemed necessary or convenient for the persecution and carrying on of the business of the corporation, and the carrying out of the objects for which it is established, and to have and to exercise all the rights, powers and privileges appertaining to corporations under the general laws of New Hampshire.

About the same time, the company began the publication of a semimonthly paper called the "Amoskeag Bulletin." In addition to printing newsworthy information on the activities of the Textile Club, the paper provided the management with a means of informing the workers of the increasing benefits provided. Finally, the paper served as a mechanism to dispense the Amoskeag philosophy, aimed at generating greater employee loyalty.

The Textile Club organized a school that provided courses in various topics, including mechanical drawing, shorthand, typing, mathematics, weaving and automobile maintenance.

The following year the company developed a comprehensive plan to improve the health and welfare of its employees and their families. In addition, the club sponsored both a glee club and a dramatic society. There was also the Amoskeag Women's Textile Club that sponsored many activities.

In 1913, the company constructed the Textile Field, complete with a stadium. To commemorate the dedication of the stadium, a baseball game was played between an all-star team from Manchester's local manufacturers' league and the Boston Red Sox. In addition, a bowling league was formed and a nine-hole golf course built for the employees. An extensive recreational program was also created for the children of Amoskeag employees. It included summer camp and scout troops for the boys and a domestic school for the girls. The company also built a playground, complete with recreational equipment and a wading pool, and provided land for children's gardens.

Amoskeag also developed a medical program that was quite extensive for the time. There was an accident department with a resident nurse and the availability of a doctor to treat industrial accidents. The company also provided a visiting nurse to tend to sick employees and their families. In that respect, the company also employed a housekeeper that would assist in the running of residences in which the homemakers were ill. Finally, the medical program provided for free dental care for all of the children of the company's employees.

In February of 1912, Treasurer Dumaine circulated a plan to the employees illustrating how a worker could become a stockholder of Amoskeag. The plan allowed employees to purchase from one to 20 shares through a $5 down payment per share. At that point the company would purchase the stock in the employee's name. Thereafter, $1 per share would be deducted from each biweekly pay envelope until the shares were paid for. Any dividend earned on the stock during that time would go to offset the total cost. Following the payoff of the loan, the stock would be turned over to the worker. The intention of the plan appears to be twofold. First, it would allow employees to share in Amoskeag's profitability. Second, it promulgated greater loyalty to the company.

Perhaps the most dramatic aspect of the benefit program was

Playground views

An official's residence

introduced on March 12, 1912, when the company initiated a program for those who had been in Amoskeag's employ for at least five years. For no money down, they could purchase house lots on the west side of the river from the corporation. Amoskeag would give the purchaser a mortgage that required neither principal nor interest payments as long as the worker remained in Amoskeag's employee. The mortgage would be subordinated to any loan that the individual was able to obtain from the local banks. This subordination allowed the employee to build his own one- or two-family home with little or nothing down.

If the individual remained employed with Amoskeag for a second five-year period, the company would surrender half of the mortgage for the payment of $1. If the employment continued for a third five-year period, then a second $1 payment would totally eliminate the land mortgage. In effect, the employee would acquire the lot for a total cost of $2.

Obviously, one intention was to create an environment in which employees would develop a long-term relationship with Amoskeag and become less willing to relocate to other New England mill towns should labor rate differences suggest such a move. On the other hand, the program is indicative of the gains made by mill workers. When the first mill was constructed on the east side of the river, workers could expect to live in boarding houses. In later years, the workers could expect to live in tenement houses. Now, the dream of owning one's own home was within the average worker's grasp.

At the same time that Amoskeag was embarking on this new approach to provide housing for its workers, it continued to maintain and improve the condition of its corporate housing. All units were subject to periodic maintenance. In 1913, it razed the remaining wooden housing units in the northern end of the mill housing. In their place, Amoskeag built five eight-unit brick overseers' apartments.

The same year, Amoskeag initiated a pension program that called for the agent to nominate elderly workers with a long history of employment. Upon approval of the board of trustees, the monthly pension was continued until the individual's death. The trustees reserved the option of altering or eliminating the pension, which was well within their rights since the employees had made no contributions to a fund. By 1922, the annual cost of the pensions was $27,000. While economic conditions within the industry prevented the addition of many new employees into the program after that year, all pensions were honored until the bankruptcy in 1936.

It is difficult in this day and age to assess the scope of the benefits provided to Amoskeag employees. On one hand, Amoskeag could be criticized for not including all employees in the pension program. On the other hand, Amoskeag could be classified as too paternalistic in the mixture of non-wage compensation given to its employees. It is important to evaluate the various programs based on the time period that they were put into effect. While company-sponsored stock savings plans are prevalent today, they were rare and almost unheard of when introduced by Dumaine.

The pension program, limited though it may have been, preceded the federal introduction of Social Security by some twenty years. Moreover, the Amoskeag program required no contributions by the employee.

The programs for free dental care and home nursing care demonstrated a corporation with a genuine interest in the welfare of its employees. The playgrounds, children gardens, boys camp program and boy scout programs reflect an interest in directing the youth of the community that is associated with governments and non-profit associations today.

Amoskeag's commitment to housing must be appreciated. Most of its original employee housing is still standing some 150 years after its construction. While much has been converted for commercial use, many current residents are proud owners or renters of "Corporate Housing." Many of the one- and two-family homes found on the city's west side today owe their existence to employees who took the opportunity to "purchase" Amoskeag lots.

In addition to the generous donations of land for city parks and churches in the nineteenth century, today many Manchester residents continue to benefit from the contributions made to the community by Amoskeag. Examples are the baseball stadium and country club constructed in the first quarter of the twentieth century.

At the same time, it is important to recognize that such programs had an intrinsic value to Amoskeag. The programs were introduced to assure that the corporation would have a workforce that was proud to be associated with the company. Amoskeag knew well that a contented workforce was a productive workforce. It was essential if textiles were to successfully compete with output from lower-wage-rate regions.

THE GREAT AMOSKEAG FLAG OF 1914

CHAPTER V

Amoskeag's Wartime Effort

While Amoskeag had reached its peak production in the previous five-year period, the five years 1916 through 1921 were the period of maximum profits. It was also the time in which it paid out its highest dollars in both wages and dividends. The company's production and sales during this period, summarized in the tables below, show an overall decline in production in excess of 25 percent.

AMOSKEAG PRODUCTION AND SALES
Cloth in millions of yards. Bags in thousands of units

Cloth and Bags Produced

Year	Cotton Worsteds	Total	Cloths	Bags
1916-1917	188.8	14.1	202.9	1,203.3
1917-1918	159.8	11.7	171.5	1,227.1
1918-1919	136.0	7.2	143.2	630.8
1919-1920	150.6	9.9	160.6	701.0
1920-1921	143.6	4.0	147.5	11.8
Totals	778.8	46.9	825.7	3,774.0

Cloth and Bags Sold

Year	Cotton and Worsted Cloth	Bags
1916-1917	200.2	1,209.6
1917-1918	183.7	1,199.9
1918-1919	139.7	632.0
1919-1920	161.5	662.7
1920-1921	146.9	82.1
Totals	832.0	3,786.3

Amoskeag Bulletin.
Published Twice a Month by the Amoskeag Textile Club
MANCHESTER, N. H., AUGUST 15, 1916
PRICE TWO CENTS
VOL. IV, NO. 16.

MEN OFF FOR PLATTSBURG
FINE TRIP TO THE CAMP
LEFT MANCHESTER LAST WEDNESDAY NIGHT ON SPECIAL TRAIN FROM BOSTON CARRYING HUNDREDS OF CITIZEN SOLDIERS

TEXTILE FAIR SEPT. 14, 15, 16
WILL USE ONE BIG TENT
CANVAS WILL STRETCH FROM WEST MERRIMACK TO MARKET STREETS UNDER WHICH FOURTH ANNUAL EXHIBIT WILL BE HELD

AMOSKEAG TEXTILE CLUB MEN AT PLATTSBURG.
Standing, left to right, Henry R. Dickson, Harold N. Snow, Horace M. Stevens, E. Clyde Luce, Henry J. Stone.
Sitting, Frank McBride, Ernest E. Simpson, Guy E. Chapman, Dean R. DeMerritt, Arthur P. Morrill.

WILL HAVE FIELD DAY
Yard League Players Big Windup for Season

BOY SCOUTS TO ENJOY HIKE
WILL GO TO GREENFIELD
CAMP TO BE PITCHED ON THE SHORE OF OTTER LAKE WHERE GOOD FISHING AND SWIMMING CAN BE HAD BY THE YOUNG FELLOWS

PLEASED WITH PICTURES
Omaha Paper Speaks Good Word for Amoskeag Movies

The Franklin Street School

Amoskeag Percher Drowned

Miss Woodbury Engaged

Kicked by a Horse

Loom Fixers' Outing

Will Shoot at Goffstown

During World War I, much of Amoskeag's manufacturing was devoted to production of government orders for fabrics for uniforms and other clothing items, barracks bags and for Red Cross yarns.

Prior to the United States officially entering into the war, Treasurer Dumaine announced in the February 15, 1917, issue of "The Amoskeag Bulletin" that the company had offered to pay the entire expense to equip a regiment in the event that war was declared on Germany.

Just prior to the United States' official entrance into the war, a defense league was formed at Amoskeag. Following the official declaration of war, the Textile Club offered its services to New Hampshire's Governor Henry Wilder Keyes. The company gave plowed land, seed and fertilizer, free of charge, for employee gardens in an attempt to support the home effort. The May 1 issue of the "Bulletin" ran an editorial entitled "Enlist Now." The following issue published two weeks later ran three related articles titled "Amoskeag Men Enlist," "Plows Are Kept at Work" and "More Flag Raising." Then the July 2 issue announced there would be no shutdown for summer vacations because the plants would be too busy filling war orders.

Management and employees of Amoskeag continued their war activities, concentrating on Red Cross and Liberty Loan campaigns. In February 1918, Superintendent W. Parker Straw received instructions from Washington that his services were needed on the War Industries Board for six months. Given the rank of major, Straw's assignment was to supervise the production and delivery of all cotton goods being made for the government in the war effort. Following completion of his assignment, he returned in December 1918 to serve as superintendent of Amoskeag.

As the following income statements show, the dollar sales volume was more than twice the level of the previous five-year period, despite the fact that the volume of production was down some 25 percent. That was the nature of production in wartime economics. More important, net income for the shareholders was almost four times as large than in the prior five-year period. A portion of this increase in net income was distributed to stockholders in the form of larger cash dividends. However, the vast majority was added to surplus or retained earnings.

While the overall financial performance in this five-year period was exceptional, it is important to consider two points. First, the larger profits were a result of an artificially high profit margin associated with the wartime production. Second, the decline in 1921 earnings was indicative of what Amoskeag could expect to experience in a postwar period characterized by increased Southern production and inevitable price deterioration. If anything, profit could be expected to decline even further in the future.

In the year ending May 31, 1919, Amoskeag made the best profit showing in its history. Its net income of $7.9 million was equal to 18.2 percent on sales and $42.97 per share on the common stock. Since dividends in that year were $1.2 million, the surplus recorded at $6.8 million should have been the increase in the equity accounts one would find by contrasting the balance sheets for the fiscal years ending May 31, 1918, and May 31, 1919. As the following table demonstrates, however, the actual increase in equity recorded in that year was $14.6 million, some $7.8 million more than justified by the reported surplus. If one assumed that this discrepancy is solely the result of an understatement of profits in fiscal year 1919, then the actual profits for that year would be almost double the amount reported. More likely, the almost $7.8 million of hidden equity would have resulted from previous years' underestimated profits.

It would be inappropriate to evaluate Amoskeag's accounting procedures based on current standards. However, it is important to note that the act of understating profits to insure conservatism in reporting and, if possible, to mitigate income tax obligations, does create a situation of incomplete market information. In such a situation, informed buyers might be able to purchase shares of the common stock from less informed sellers at a price substantially below its true value. Equally as important, such a situation could foster an environment where an outsider, with an appreciation of the understatement of the accounts, might succeed in acquiring a dominant position in the stock at a discounted price with the intention of profiting from the liquidation of the organization.

While the recognition of the hidden current assets in 1919 reduced the confusion on the part of the financial market as to the current worth of Amoskeag stock, the company continued its practice of not

Amoskeag Income Account
$1,000s

	1916-17	1917-18	1918-19	1919-20	1920-21
Sales	$ 30,439	$ 49,458	$ 44,016	$ 56,320	$ 31,287
Expenses	29,105	44,405	36,071	51,951	30,014
Net Income	1,334	5,053	7,945	4,369	1,273
Dividends	1,037	1,037	1,166	1,685	2,524
Surplus or (Deficit)	$ 297	$ 4,016	$ 6,779	$ 2,684	($ 1,251)
Income/Sales	4.4%	10.2%	18.1%	7.8%	4.1%
Earnings per Common Share	$ 4.72	$ 26.24	$ 42.97	$ 11.33*	$ 2.37*

*On 345,600 instead of 172,800 shares outstanding as a result of 100 percent stock dividend. On old per-share basis, earnings would have been $22.66 and $4.74

Amoskeag Balance Sheet
(May 31, 1917-21)
$1,000s

	1917	1918	1919	1920	1921
Assets					
Real Estate & Machinery	$ 3,000	$ 3,000	$ 3,000	$ 3,000	$ 3,000
Current Assets	15,953	20,417	37,163	39,522	37,455
Totals	$ 18,953	$ 23,417	$ 40,163	$ 42,522	$ 40,455
Liabilities					
Accounts Payable	$ 5,409	$ 515	$2,683	$ 1,819	$ 280
Reserves & Profit & Loss	13,544	22,902	37,480	40,703	40,175
Totals	$ 18,953	$ 23,417	$ 10,163	$ 42,522	$ 40,455
Net Working Capital	$ 10,544	$ 19,902	$ 34,480	$ 37,703	$ 37,175

capitalizing new plants and equipment. The total value on the books for the investments in real estate and machinery continued to be recorded at a nominal value of $3 million. While the magnitude of this understatement far exceeded the amount of hidden current assets that were now brought to light, the danger of this understatement of fixed assets was less dangerous since the prudent investor had two alternative means of attempting to assess the value of this portion of the company. First, the investor could estimate the value based on benchmarks as to the value per spindle. Using this approach, at $50 per spindle, the plant was worth some $37 million. A second approach would be to use the City of Manchester's property evaluation which was about $30.5 million in 1921.

This assessment of Amoskeag's property represented 27.7 percent of Manchester's total valuation and resulted in a property tax obligation to the city of $748,300. This was a substantially higher figure than the company would have had to pay if its plants were taxed at a rate equal to Southern mills, or, for that matter, at a rate equal to that found in the other five New England states. While the essential community services supported by the City of Manchester could not have been taken care of if its property tax had been as low as the rates which prevailed in the South, Amoskeag was at a disadvantage over other Northern mills. The chief difference in the company's tax load as compared to the rest of New England was in the stock-in-trade tax in force in New Hampshire.

Because of the five-for-one stock split (three common and two preferred) in the 1911 restructuring and the subsequent 100 percent stock dividend in 1920 on the three shares of common, it is difficult to appreciate the gains experienced by an Amoskeag investor who had purchased the stock prior to 1911 and was still holding the shares in 1921. For this reason, the following table has been constructed based on the original 57,000 shares issued when the Amory and Manchester Mills were merged with Amoskeag in 1906.

At the time of the 1906 merger, the stock was selling for about $300. At the peak in 1921 the aggregate value of the eight shares that represented each original share was in excess of $800 ($109 for each of the six shares of common and $80 for each of the two shares of preferred). Do not lose sight of the fact that if one extracts the 1918

Amoskeag Profitability
for Fiscal Years 1907-1921

	Company Totals in 1,000s			Per Share Adjusted for Splits		
Year	Earnings	Dividends	Surplus	Earnings	Dividends	Surplus
1907	$ 1,232	$ 922	$ 310	$ 21.39	$ 16.00	$ 5.59
1908	1,251	922	329	21.72	16.00	5.72
1909	782	691	91	13.58	12.00	1.58
1910	761	691	70	13.21	12.00	1.21
1911	722	691	31	12.53	12.00	.53
1912	1,104	1,037	67	19.17	18.00	1.17
1913	1,062	1,037	26	18.44	18.00	.44
1914	1,023	1,037	(14)	17.76	18.00	(.24)
1915	1,079	1,037	43	18.73	18.00	.73
1916	1,179	1,037	143	20.47	18.00	2.47
1917	1,334	1,037	297	23.16	18.00	5.16
1918	5,053	1,037	4,016	87.72	18.00	69.72
1919	7,945	1,166	6,779	137.93	20.24	117.69
1920	4,369	1,685	2,684	75.85	29.25	46.60
1921	1,273	2,524	(1,251)	22.10	43.82	(21.72)

through 1920 earnings associated with wartime production, the reported earnings showed little long-term growth. The 1921 profit of $1,272,000 was virtually identical to the 1907 value of $1,232,000. At the same time, it is important to remember there was consensus that the reported earnings for the later years presented in this table might severely underestimate actual income.

Most important, similar wartime profits experienced by Southern competitors provided these producers with the capital to increase capacity. Amoskeag and the other Northern textile mills needed to address the labor cost differential.

When Amoskeag's 1920-21 fiscal year began, the textile industry had passed its peak. In the next few months there was increasing evidence that the postwar boom was nearing its end. Management was once again faced with the critical issue as to the proper balance between its obligation to its stockholders and its obligations to its workers and its host community. To a great extent, the wartime profit opportunities delayed this inevitable decision. Amoskeag not only had to deal with an overall decline in the demand in textiles, it also had the particular problem of the loss of favor of ginghams, Amoskeag's most important product line.

The average number of employees at Amoskeag was 12,076 in 1919, or more than 47 percent of all the industrial workers in Manchester. The company's largest payroll year was from October 1919 to September 1920, when a total of $14.75 million was distributed in wages, more than double that of the 10 years before.

The dollar rise was a result of frequent advances in wage rates during this same time period. In this respect, Amoskeag increases mirrored other New England firms all fighting for labor to meet wartime demand and the high national inflation rate. Increases of 7 1/2 percent were announced in May and October 1917; 10 percent in April 1918; and 12 1/2 percent in June of the same year. Because the increase had been 15 percent elsewhere, Amoskeag employees went on strike in July, called by the United Textile Workers. This was the first trade union strike at Amoskeag since 1886, when the Knights of Labor were unsuccessful. Since eleven departments of the company were on war orders at the time, the Secretary of War dispatched an arbitrator. The strike was settled in five days with an award of an additional increase in wages to make the total 15 percent. The union added 5,000 new members as a result, and in the succeeding four years it was a factor in employer-employee relations. The management met with representatives of the Manchester Textile Council (ten locals) and established an adjustment board to meet with grievance committees set up by union members in each department, but there was no arrangement for union check off of dues or of closed or preferential shop. Future disputes went to the Federal War Board.

In his annual message in 1917, Governor Henry W. Keyes of New Hampshire advocated the reduction of the workweek from 55 to 54 hours. The February issue of the "Bulletin" carried an editorial on "Question of the Hour" signed by Agent H. F. Straw.

Mr. Straw called attention to some of the problems of Amoskeag at that time. He said that the climate and other physical conditions of New Hampshire were the least favorable to cotton spinning of any state. Its mills had to pay the highest amounts for freight, cotton and coal and for shipping goods to New York and the West. He declared that the cost of labor was the most important factor in competition with Southern mills, which averaged two-thirds of the wages paid by Amoskeag. He stated that the reduction of one hour a week seemed small, but it would cost someone in New Hampshire, either employer or employees, $300,000 a year.

Mr. Straw also pointed out that while in New Hampshire cotton spindles had increased by 155,991 from 1906 to 1916, gains were 1,530,973 in North Carolina and 1,239,129 in South Carolina. He explained that the greater part of the increase in New Hampshire was due to the building of the Coolidge Mill. Otherwise, the New Hampshire gain in cotton spindles was barely 3 percent. It is intriguing that by 1921 the number of cotton spindles in the South already represented 85.4 percent of the number installed in New England, where a total of 18.4 million was reached in that year. This reference to Southern competition is especially interesting, as it became an increasingly important problem for the company in the following years. Amoskeag would become the last of the large textile mills in New England to succumb to increasing costs and Southern competition. The war probably had the effect of postponing needed readjustments at the mills and the inevitable day of reckoning. Regardless of opposition to the 54-hour law by Amoskeag and other New Hampshire mills, the measure passed and became effective January 1, 1918.

In May 1919, the Manchester Textile Council requested a 15 percent wage effective June 2. Within a week the company acceded to the request, with the stipulation that the agreement remain in force to the third Monday in April 1920. However, on December 1, 1919, the company gave its employees a voluntary 12 1/2 percent increase in wages "due to the continued increase in the cost of necessities," although the production of the mills had declined 16 percent in the twelve months ending November 30, 1919. A day or two before Christmas, 5 percent was paid on all yearly salaries with a promise of a similar amount on June 1, 1920, if the present rate of wages remained unchanged. This was really a 10 percent increase in salary payable in two installments. On May 29, 1920, a 15 percent increase in wages became effective.

After July, 1920 the price trend was definitely downward. The reprieve that New England mills received because of wartime demand was over. Amoskeag, again, needed to address its competitive situation relative to Southern mills. By July, the worsted section was closed down completely. By October, the cotton weaving department was reduced to a three-day schedule. Prices of ginghams, napped goods, shirtings, tickings and denims were slashed by one-third. A second price cut was announced in December, at which time the entire cotton section was placed on a three-day week.

When W. Parker Straw, who succeeded his father as agent in June 1920, announced that all departments of the company would resume operations Monday, January 3, 1921, after the December closing. He explained that the sole object of the price reductions was to attract business to be able to keep the mill operational. A new wage scale calling for a 22 1/2 percent reduction, the same as in other New England mills, was put into effect. Agent Straw explained the company's position further by pointing out that they could not start at full capacity because the company had no new orders, but whatever goods were made would be stored to meet anticipated demand. The strategy was to operate half time, three days a week, until further notice. Full-time manufacturing would resume as soon as conditions warranted.

In March 1921, quotations on napped goods, which had risen in the latter part of 1919 and early 1920 along with other cotton goods, were cut from 37 1/2 to 12 1/2 cents a yard.

From 1914 to 1918 wage-rate changes had kept pace with the rising cost of living. In 1919 wage rate increases exceeded the cost of living index. This divergence increased in 1920 and became considerable in 1921, despite the 22 1/2 percent wage reduction in that year. In effect, after the 1921 wage cut, workers' real wage, earnings adjusted for cost of living changes, were higher than at the beginning of this five-year period.

Prior to the 1921 wage cut, management had tried to make Amoskeag's labor costs competitive with the South by increasing the work load. In March 1920, the management wanted to increase the number of frames tended by warpers from three to seven, but the union insisted that workers should not run more than three because of the impact on the quality of the production. Piece rates were substituted for hourly rates for hand folders in September 1920, to make possible a 25 percent increase in production with a resulting gain of the same amount in wages. The agent said that the existing method of limiting production was economically wrong and "that this nation wouldn't get ahead if everybody loafed on the job."

Later in the year, the union reported that loom fixers in the worsted section "were being driven to death." The Adjustment Board met in October to determine whether worsted weavers would be justified in registering a complaint concerning the six-loom experimental job. Two months later, the status of this situation was illustrated by the statement of the union representative to the board, advising "that he thought that the final solution of the six-loom problem would probably be for the weavers to hold a meeting and 'tell the management to go to hell,' as far as the six-loom set was concerned." Greater production by doffers was attempted by increasing the number of sides tended from 50 to 56. All of this illustrates some of the disputes with labor that created increasingly difficult conditions for the company in its efforts to assure efficiency and reduce costs.

Management and labor relations were now in perilous strain. The ultimate cause of the nine-month strike of 1922 was yet to come.

STRIKERS OUTSIDE THE MILL GATES

CHAPTER VI

The Strike of 1922

The 1922 strike at Amoskeag lasted more than nine months, from February 13 to November 25, and resulted in a loss of about $9 million in wages and the loss of considerable business to competitors that was never regained. The effects of the strike on labor relations and plant operations in Manchester continued up to the time of the liquidation of the company in 1936. The strike was in response to management's attempt to reduce the hourly wage rate by 20 percent and to increase the workweek to 54 hours to be in a better position to compete with Southern mills. This 20 percent reduction was in addition to the 22.5 percent reduction in effect since January 3, 1921.

Management throughout New England held that the wage rate reduction was necessary to bring Northern labor costs in line with the South. In those states not handicapped by legislation restricting the workweek, the mills also wanted to increase the working hours on a par with the South. This would be of value to the mills once they returned to capacity operation because it would lower the fixed plant costs per unit of output when machines would be operating more hours per week.

On February 2, 1922, when Amoskeag announced the 20 percent wage reduction and the increase in the workweek from 48 to 54 hours, Agent W. Parker Straw called attention to the fact that his company's workers would have only a 10 percent reduction in their pay envelopes, as compared to a full 20 percent for those in other states, such as Massachusetts where hours were shorter. The new schedule would start February 13 at 6:45 a.m., allow one hour at noon and then continue to 5:30 p.m.

Amoskeag was trying in every way possible to meet competition. It was stated at the time that under the new schedules the company hoped to have several months, at least, of full operation. Wages in the South, where the workweek averaged 55 to 60 hours, were 40 percent below those in the North. Because mills in the North had no control over prices of cotton, wool, coal or taxes, the one possibility for savings was in labor costs.

While the unions were preparing to take a strike vote, the newspapers of the city were advising caution on the part of the workers. They were urged not to resort to violence and disorder. Any such action might lead to the mills' closing permanently, which would be a disaster for their families and for the whole community.

United Textile Workers' (UTW) National Vice President James Starr and other union officials came to Manchester to lead the "fight to the finish." Meanwhile, efforts were being made by local civic organizations and Catholic pastors to prevent a strike. There was even a suggestion that the intervention of the United States government might be sought. The unions and textile council started taking a strike vote on February 5. The results of the balloting, announced in the newspapers on February 10, showed that the wage cut and increase in hours had been rejected by 99 percent of the 12,150 votes cast. All organized employees were ordered not to report for work. Amoskeag had 15,500 on its payrolls and the Stark 1,400, the voters represented only 73 percent of the total. The French language newspaper "L'Avenir" questioned the results and voting methods used. It declared that of the 17,000 employees in the two mills, hardly one-fourth belonged to the unions. If the facts were really known, added "L'Avenir," it would be found that probably no more than 3,500 votes in all were cast in favor of a strike, and it suggested that a committee of citizens be permitted to count the votes.

When the results of the vote were made known to him, Agent Straw insisted there could be no compromise. He repeated that the new schedule was the least possible adjustment that the company could make. The decision of the employees to vote a strike was to be regretted, he said, but promised that the mills would open to give work to those who cared to accept the new conditions and recognized the futility of delay and consequent loss in wages. The economic situation was beyond the mills' control, he asserted.

Monday morning, February 13, the mill gates were picketed while Amoskeag and Stark employees started the first day of the longest strike Manchester had ever known. Fewer than a hundred employees reported for work at Amoskeag on that day. The mills had to be closed. Agent Straw, in his notice announcing the shutdown, stated that the workers would be duly advised when the company should decide to reopen. Vice President Starr promised orderly picketing. The union Strategy Board appointed captains and plans were made for daily meetings of the workers.

Various attempts were under way soon after the strike started to arrange for mediation of the Manchester labor troubles. Local ministers conferred with Agent Straw to hear the mills' arguments as a basis for suggesting a compromise settlement. Manchester aldermen, who wanted to help bring an end to the strike, invited both parties to attend a conference that might lead to a profitable peace. The importance of an early end to the strike was continuously emphasized in local pulpits. Two federal conciliators arrived in Manchester to probe the situation through consultations with mill officials and union leaders. Thomas McMahon, president of the UTW, asked the American Federation of Labor, with which it was affiliated, to seek a congressional investigation of the situation, and the strikers at Manchester, on their own account, asked Congress to investigate. The Manchester Central Labor Union appointed a committee to confer with Senator Moses of New Hampshire to help the matter along. When no reply came from Congress, it was promptly "flayed" by the strikers. Later Vice President Starr said there would be no attempt to probe the strike. He said he was well satisfied with the progress already made and that "money was pouring in" for the strike fund.

When UTW President Thomas McMahon came to Manchester at the end of February, he first said the workers would never arbitrate the matter of pay and hours. At a mass meeting at which various speakers were heard, he later modified this position and said they would arbitrate on wages but not on hours. The hours principle would not be sacrificed, he declared. He praised the strikers' stand on law and order and said that "everything points to a successful fight." Following President McMahon's visit, all day picketing was ordered, starting March 1.

Early in March, Agent W. Parker Straw addressed a letter to the people of New Hampshire that was run in all the leading newspapers. Its purpose was to explain the "Question at Issue." He called attention to the fact that over the past 20 years, while the South's number of cotton spindles had increased over 190 percent the North had only experienced 41 percent growth. The primary reason that Southern mills were gaining a larger share of the market was their labor cost advantage as a result of longer hours and lower hourly wage rates. The agent reminded the people of New Hampshire that Amoskeag had always paid, and hoped to continue to pay, higher wages and have shorter hours, but unusual difficulties were compelling curtailment all over New England.

Amoskeag, Mr. Straw said, was owned by 3,700 persons, 1,500 of whom lived in New Hampshire. Since 1831, the company had paid the City of Manchester $215 million in wages and $8.5 million in taxes.

As for the strike, the agent said that while it was reported that more than 12,000 voted in favor to strike, there was general understanding that only 3,500 voted. He emphasized that each week of idleness meant a loss of $300,000 in wages.

In conclusion, he promised that when a sufficient number of operatives desired to return, management would reopen the employment department and be ready to receive applications. He said it was Amoskeag's desire to continue to operate in New Hampshire and pay the best wages possible to meet the prices of competitive products. The company wanted peace and prosperity for itself and for the community. To attain the objective, the cooperation of the workers and all of the citizens of the state was necessary.

In response, a series of six statements were published in the same New Hampshire papers by the UTW, under the direction of Vice President James Starr.

The first statement, titled "An Excuse Not a Reason," said that prior to the February wage cut there had been no substantial change in the relative weekly pay between the North and the South. The union contended that if one adds the cost for maintaining Southern mill villages, as calculated by the American Cotton Manufacturing Association (ACMA), then there was virtually no difference in labor costs between the two regions. The union argued that if the North were successful in lowering wages in New England, then the South would respond by lowering its wages.

If the village cost, again as calculated by the ACMA, represented a correct estimate of operating in the South, then there would be little to support Amoskeag's position. However, in addressing the cost of maintaining Southern mill villages, the association ignored the fact that Amoskeag, through the payment of property taxes, was making similar payments to the support of Manchester.

The union's second published statement, "Results of Southern Competition," concentrated on past profits of Amoskeag. The article posed that during the recent past Amoskeag had been highly profitable and paid generous dividends, that in the last 10 years, 1912 to 1921, when Southern competition had been keenest, Amoskeag made annual profits 7 3/4 times as great as in 1885 to 1901. The statement failed to comment on the increased size of Amoskeag and the ability in the future to maintain the higher wartime profit levels.

"Vital to Every Citizen," the third letter, contrasted the growth in earnings and dividends relative to wages for the prior 10 years. The statement demonstrated that before the proposed wage decrease, wages grew at a rate similar to profits, but that dividends grew at a much greater percentage. This statement, as well as the previous one, may be indicative of poor timing on the part of New England mills' attempt to bring wages in line with the South. If they had waited two years, following inevitable losses, their position might have been more readily received by the workers.

In the fourth weekly statement, "The Real Competition," the union concentrated on the issue of the relatively low wages in the textile industry. They pointed out that the cost of living in the North was higher than in the South.

Before the present wage cut, cotton mill wages in the North and

South were at a level that would not yield enough in 52 full-time weeks per year to furnish income sufficient for workers in the industry, skilled and unskilled, to meet the cost of living as determined by any budget, ever priced, even by the employers themselves. These statistics, in human terms, mean this: If there is a family, the wife or children of a man working in a cotton mill must also work in the mills to maintain existence at the lowest level or mere substance.

While convincing, it would have been advantageous for the workers to pursue this argument to its ultimate conclusion. In an industry experiencing overcapacity, before there can be a substantial increase in the standard of living of the workers, some producers must be driven out of business. Ultimately, wages in Southern firms in the 40's and 50's were higher because of Amoskeag's demise.

In "Life and Death," the fifth statement, the union attacked the corporation's position on the workweek. The union held that Amoskeag's comparison of spindle-hours worked was not justifiable because, as Southern mills concentrated on goods that could be produced for stock, Amoskeag produced goods that were more seasonal. Second, the statement pointed out that the value of Northern workers' output exceeded that of their Southern counterparts. Finally, the union disputed Amoskeag's concentration on the "narrow profit margin" by illustrating a profit per dollar of sale of 5.5 percent.

Published on April 1, the final statement called "The Beneficial Interest" again cited past Amoskeag profits. Here the emphasis was placed on the fact that since 1907 all growth had been through retained earnings, despite the generous dividends paid out. The statement then contrasted the growth in the stockholder's investment with the earnings of the mill worker and presented the following challenge to the stockholder:

> Upon the stockholders of Amoskeag who received Amoskeag profits rests ultimately the responsibility for Amoskeag policy. Are the stockholders satisfied with the division which is made of "the beneficial interest" in the business between those who invest money and those who invest labor? It is right that the stockholders should assume that question, each for himself "For onto whomsoever much is given, of him shall be much required."

As the strike progressed, the local union leaders, through their Strategy Board, planned a campaign of relief for the strikers. The program included several "tag days." At the one held on the third of March, 20,000 tags were sold to raise funds to help the strikers. City doctors, druggists and merchants did everything they could to help the workers. The New Hampshire Furniture Co. held a clearance sale for UTW workers. The Star Furniture Co. arranged for a whist party and dance for the strikers' benefit. The strikers received cooperation not only locally, but from other parts of the state and even from outside of New Hampshire. Mrs. Glendower Evans, a wealthy Brookline, Mass., resident and an Amoskeag stockholder, offered cash to the strikers and sent speakers to help their cause. One of the interesting developments during the early part of the strike was the offer of homes for the idle workers in Ontario and Quebec. On March 3, sixty families, consisting of 312 people, left Manchester for Quebec.

The management of Stark, like most mills in New England, had adopted a similar wage policy as Amoskeag. The Stark employees were also on strike. International Cotton, the corporation that now owned the Stark Mill, was interested in disposing of this location to concentrate its production in its Southern mills. The purchase of the Stark by Amoskeag was a logical development and had been considered a possibility for years. It was completely surrounded by Amoskeag properties and, prior to the sale in 1901, had been under the control of Amoskeag investors. At the end of May 1922, when Treasurer Dumaine made what was called a "casual visit" to the Stark plant, the frequently reported story that Amoskeag planned to buy it was revived. Following a June 1 meeting of the directors of International Cotton Mills, it was announced that the sale would take place.

Amoskeag had agreed that upon delivery of the deed for the properties, it would pay $1.9 million to International Cotton Mills and the balance of the purchase price on determination of the market value of the personal property, including all inventories. The second check was for $700,000, which made a total price of $2.6 million. Amoskeag was probably one of the few textile manufacturing corporations in a position to make such an acquisition. It is interesting to recall for comparative purposes that when Sidney Coolidge sold the Stark to

Consolidated Duck Co., he got only $1.8 million for the whole business, including $1.2 million of net current. Of course, the properties were in much better condition in 1922. The equipment then included good carding and hundreds of new Draper looms, worth at that time about $400 each.

This acquisition completed Amoskeag's attempt, begun in 1906 with the merging of the Manchester and the Amory mills, to absorb the four big mills in Manchester under one corporate headquarters. This was the first important property addition to Amoskeag since the building of the 102,000 spindle Coolidge Mill in 1909.

On June 1, the company announced that it would open its biggest plant, the Coolidge Mill, also that other mills would be opened when there was both a demand for the output and a supply of workers willing to accept the wage rate and hours of work. Only 100 operatives returned to work at Coolidge on Monday, June 5. A large gathering of strikers was on hand and the entire police force found it hard to keep the crowds moving. One half hour after the gates were opened they were immediately closed again. The number of operatives had increased to 300 in a few days and there was a steady gain during the rest of the month.

On July 1, a citizen's committee met with Treasurer Dumaine about the situation, suggesting that a conference between the two parties would be desirable. They were told that the corporation was ready then, as always, to meet a committee of its employees at any time, but it had no intention of receding from its original position of 54 hours a week and a 20 percent reduction in wages. With an improvement in the wool situation Amoskeag started to operate 25 worsted looms in the woolen mills.

Efforts to end the strike continued. It was suggested that the issue be submitted to the State Board of Conciliation and Arbitration, but the company insisted that a 54-hour work week and a 20 percent cut in wages were necessary for successful operation and the strikers refused to arbitrate on hours. By July 26, with Amoskeag's cotton and worsted departments operating in a limited way, between 1,400 and 1,500 workers were now employed and 10 percent of the cotton looms were running. The situation led to the opinion by some that the cotton mills could not win out except by a compromise solution.

By August 2 Amoskeag had 2,800 of 20,500 looms in the cotton section in operation. Approximately 2,000 workers were now at work, and applications from 500 other employees had been received. During the rest of the month conditions steadily improved, with more and more machinery being put into operation. On August 22, when the Langdon Mills were reopened in part, only a small number applied for work.

On Labor Day the union held a parade. Estimates of marchers ran from 4,300 to 8,000, despite the fact that the entire day was met with a drizzling rain.

At this point it might be well to assess the state of the strike. After seven months, some 2,500 out of the 17,000 labor force, including the Stark mills, had decided to accept Amoskeag's original February 13 wage rate and work week. Over the entire period there was very little violence — to the great credit of both sides.

Near the end of August, Pacific Mills at Lawrence, Mass., offered to rescind the 20 percent wage cut that had been in effect for over six months. Over the next two weeks other mills in New England followed its lead. On September 10, Agent Straw announced:

> The Amoskeag Company, in accordance with its policy of paying a wage equal to that paid in communities comparable with Manchester, following at once the recently announced action of the mills in Maine, operating on a 54 hour basis by advancing its wage scale (back to the pre-February 2 rate) effective Monday, September 11. The running time of this mill will remain unchanged, fifty-four hours per week.

Whether the wage rate concession in Maine triggered a response on the part of Amoskeag in fear of losing its labor force to other New England firms who had returned to the 1921 wage levels, or whether it simply proved to be a convenient excuse to reduce demands in a labor dispute that was both longer and more costly than anticipated, is difficult to determine. In either event, the collective position on New England mills to reduce wages had eroded.

In response to the Amoskeag announcement, Vice President Starr of the UTW stated:

> I recommend to the workers that they take no step on the propo-
> sition until they get together at a meeting and vote. As the 48
> hours is one of the main issues of the fight, I would advise the
> workers to wait, get together and decide.

He warned them that if they went back to work under the current stated conditions, the company could cut wages at a later point and end up winning everything.

The "Manchester Union," one of the city's two leading newspapers, recommended that the workers return to work, noting that since they would be paid for the extra six hours, their pay would be even higher than before the February 2 announcement. On September 12, a union meeting was held at the Strand Theater where almost all of the approximately 2,000 in attendance voted to continue the strike.

By October 17, Amoskeag had 4,500 people at work. Applications were being received at the rate of 200 to 500 a week. A few days later it was announced that the company now had 7,000 looms in operation. The big bag mill of the northern division was opened October 23 with more than 300 looms in operation. There had been a gain of 600 workers during the previous week. All departments were showing increases. No. 9 Mill was opened October 24, bringing the number of looms in operation up to 8,000. Scores of Polish operatives applied for their former jobs. Union leaders sent four pickets to the employment department to attempt to check the continuing break in their ranks. The weaving room at Amory Mill resumed, in part, on October 30. The company had started 1,100 looms during the week.

In October, more definite efforts were made to end the strike. Mayor Tindel of Manchester appointed a committee of 10 to confer with Amoskeag officials and strike leaders. It included two members of the union Strategy Board, as well as business and professional men. Treasurer Dumaine and Agent Straw and representatives of the strikers' executive board were invited to meet with the committee on October 13. On that same day the strikers received a letter from Mrs. Glendower Evans, Brookline, Mass., an Amoskeag stockholder, urging them to continue the fight for the 48-hour week. Following the suggestion of the citizen's committee, representatives of the company and a committee of former employees planned to meet in joint conference, but the union's committee refused to attend because two Amoskeag employees who had already returned to work had been invited by the agent to attend the meeting. The union voted to continue the 48-hour fight.

The next attempt at a settlement of the strike, now in its thirty-seventh week, was a meeting organized by Bishop George Albert Guertin of the New Hampshire Catholic Diocese. A joint conference of Bishop Guertin, Agent Straw and a committee of strikers was held October 25 at the Catholic Rectory. It was the first meeting of the two parties to the dispute. A compromise proposal of the bishop for a 51-hour week was voted on by seventeen textile unions and approved. When the result of the balloting was reported to the bishop on November 1, it was made known that the company had rejected the compromise. The proposal had stipulated that the 51-hour schedule should be continued to February 1, 1923, when officials of the company should meet representatives of the workers and determine by agreement whether or not conditions or other circumstances warranted the restoration of the 48-hour week.

When over 600 applied for their former jobs on Thursday and Friday, November 2 and 3, it represented the biggest gain since the strike started. By this time 8,300 of Amoskeag's looms were in operation. There were then skeleton crews in 17 of the 20 main mills. It was expected that there would be a rush of workers now that the Guertin compromise had failed. In fact, on Monday, November 6, hundreds more applied for jobs. As the result of further breaks in the union ranks of Polish and French workers, the company put 1,000 more looms in operation, bringing the total to 10,000. The carding and spinning departments of Mill No. 1 in the central division reopened November 8. This was the eighteenth main mill to start operations since the controversy started. Additional looms were also put into operation at this time. Three more departments were opened November 13 and 1,600 more looms started operation. One thousand additional applications for work were received. Scores were turned away because there were no jobs available. With the opening of No. 12 on the same day, all main mills were operating in part, except the Jefferson. Extra help was sent to the employment department to handle the crowd. The next day, November 14, the spinning and carding rooms at Jefferson were opened. This meant that all of Amoskeag's 20 mills were now producing in part. Fifty percent of the company's looms were in operation and approximately 7,000 people had returned to work. More than 1,000 looms were started up November 20 and 500 more workers applied for their former jobs. The next day crowds were at the employment bureau again. The total gains for the week were 1,500 looms and 800 operators reemployed, the latter making a total of 8,000 workers out of the normal 17,000. By the end of the month, the number had increased to 9,000. The strike was finally called off November 25, but under protest.

Developments leading up to the end of the strike had started November 15, when a committee of former employees met in conference with Amoskeag officials and received the terms under which operatives still on strike might return. The company required the acceptance of the 54-hour weekly schedule and the wage scale that had been in effect before the strike started on February 13. The company said it would not take back employees who had been guilty of violence or intimidation, or whose conduct during the strike had been such as to destroy the possibility of maintaining the relations of employer and employee with mutual respect and confidence. It was added that the management would be glad to receive at any time a committee of employees to discuss matters of mutual interest. Additional work rooms would be reopened one at a time, and it would probably be January before the plants could return to normal operations. Only those formerly employed in each would be allowed to apply for work there. The unions devoted three days of balloting on the company's terms and on November 21 it was announced that 99 percent had voted against acceptance. It was understood, however, that fewer than 3,000 voted. But four days later, on Nov. 25, representatives of the 10 unions recommended that the former workers return to work under protest and the strike was called off. Union leaders said that very little discrimination was being shown against those who had participated in the strike. They planned to continue relief work for at least six weeks until all former workers had been given jobs. With the end of the long strike, one prominent textile observer said:

> The whole industry owes Amoskeag a debt. The position taken
> by the management was the best thing for the operatives as well

as the owners. It contributed substantially to saving textile manufacturing in New Hampshire. A 48-hour week would have been harmful to every individual and industry in the state.

Because of a nearly 10-month strike, cotton and worsted cloth production at Amoskeag in the fiscal years ended May 31, 1922 and 1923 amounted to only 132.5 and 116.5 million yards. Sales in the latter year were only 96 million yards. The decline in sales resulting from unfavorable market conditions, increasing manufacturing costs and Southern competition seriously affected Amoskeag's earning capacity. It had already shown a substantial deficit after dividends in 1921. From 1922 to 1925 the company continued to show large deficits after dividends. The total loss in surplus for the four years was over $9 million. The figures would have been larger if it were not for the interest earned on Amoskeag's liquid investments.

In the four fiscal years 1921-1925 Amoskeag produced about 477 million yards of cotton and worsted cloth. No bags had been made since 1921. The average annual cloth production of 119 million yards in the current period compared with 165 million yards in the preceding five years and the peak of 220 million yards in 1911-1916. The 1921-1925 production was distributed between cotton and worsted cloth as shown below.

As in preceding periods, ginghams constituted the largest single item in Amoskeag's production. During the four years the percentages were as follows: 1922 - 52 percent; 1923 - 52 percent; 1924 - 49 percent; and, 1925 - 37 percent. They were, of course, also making napped goods, chambrays, bleached madras, crash towelings, denims, sheetings and worsted dress goods. Among the worsteds were serges, cheviots and panamas.

The chief production problem after 1924 was to find substitutes for gingham. The seriousness of the situation became particularly acute in 1925. The company was developing plans for the production of other fabrics to insure complete operation of its tremendous spinning and weaving equipment. In the latter part of August 1925, it was reported that Amoskeag would soon offer "rayonized" fabrics. They were said to comprise three lines, handsome in appearance and likely to result in a distinct stimulation to sales. It was added that if they

AMOSKEAG MANUFACTURING CO.
COTTON AND WORSTED CLOTHS PRODUCED

(June 1, 1921 to May 31, 1925)

Year (Ended May 31)	Cotton (million yards)	Worsted (million yards)	Total (million yards)
1922	125.4	7.2	132.6
1923	110.3	6.2	116.5
1924	130.5	7.8	138.3
1925	84.5	5.1	89.6
Totals	450.7	26.3	477.0

proved successful, Amoskeag planned to make its own rayon yarn. At the time, the company's mills were operating at only 60 percent of capacity.

Beginning with 1924, Amoskeag built up a good business in automobile fabrics for tops, side curtains and seat coverings. It sold substantial quantities to Ford, General Motors and Hudson. A man was hired to be in Detroit to keep in touch with the auto trade. At one time, the company had 150 looms operating day and night producing auto fabrics.

Amoskeag also made linen suitings. Another product was 25 percent flax toweling. Diaper cloths were produced later under the trade names Lullaby and Peekaboo.

Sales for the four years totalled $105 million but there was a net loss for the period of $2.7 million. A total of $6.7 million in dividends was distributed during the four years, a final total deficit of $ 9.5 million.

Recall that in the preceding period (1916-1921), sales totalled $212 million and the net income was $20 million. After the payment of $7.5 million in dividends there was an increase of $12.5 million in surplus. Apparently the losses of 1921-1925 almost wiped out the wartime increases in surplus.

When Amoskeag increased the number of shares of no par common to 365,600 on May 7, 1920, the stock was put on a $1.50 quarterly basis, which was continued until November 1922. Payments were then reduced to $1 and finally to 75 cents in February 1923. No dividends on this issue were paid after August 2, 1924. The semiannual of $2.25 was paid regularly on the preferred until February 2, 1926.

The income account of the Amoskeag Manufacturing Company for the four years between June 1, 1921, and May 31, 1925, compares as follows:

COMPARATIVE INCOME ACCOUNT

(June 1, 1921 to May 31, 1925)

$ 1,000s

	1921-1922	1922-1923	1923-1924	1924-1925
Sales	$24,839	$22,162	$33,164	$25,200
Expenses	24,191	22,237	36,015	25,656
Net Income	$ 648	($ 75)	($ 2,851)	($ 456)
Dividends	2,524	2,005	1,487	709
Surplus or (Deficit)	($ 1,876)	($ 2,080)	($ 4,338)	($ 1,165)

An analysis of the factors involved in the profit accounts of the Amoskeag Manufacturing Company in these four years clearly shows how it was handicapped by the high cost of cotton manufacturing in that period. It was well known that Amoskeag had a large income from investments. The company's policy for many years had been to set aside half of its income for plant improvement and profitable investment, including Liberty Bonds and other government securities, as first noted in the 1923 and 1924 statements, which yielded up to $1 million annually. Had this income not been included in the figures above, the losses would have been greater.

As different balance sheet arrangements were used by Amoskeag in 1925 after the formation of a holding company, only the figures for 1922-1924 are presented. In the balance sheets the Amoskeag plant is still valued at the nominal $3,000,000, even though the company's properties in this period included the Stark Mills and the company's new $1 million hydroelectric development completed in 1923. It was a fairly general opinion that the manufacturing properties could not be replaced for less than $50 million. During the tax suit in 1924, the reproduction cost of Amoskeag plants was estimated at $62.3 million and the depreciated value at $42.4 million.

The tremendous size of Amoskeag has been illustrated in many

BALANCE SHEET
(FOR YEARS ENDED MAY 31)
$1,000s

	1921-1922	1922-1923	1923-1924
Assets			
Plant	$ 3,000	$ 3,000	$ 3,000
Current Assets	35,680	36,648	41,782
Total Assets	$ 38,680	$ 39,648	$ 44,782
Claims			
Liabilities	$ 6,250	$ 6,350	$ 14,750
Equity	32,430	33,298	30,032
Total Claims	$ 38,680	$ 39,648	$ 44,782
Net Current Assets	$ 29,430	$ 30,298	$ 27,032

ways. It was the largest cotton manufacturing plant in the world and represented 3 percent of this country's textile industry. Amoskeag's share of the ginghams and colored goods, on which the company concentrated, was closer to 15 percent of the national market. One stockholder, who was well acquainted with textile manufacturing, decided during this period to go all through the whole property, "not down every aisle of preparatory, weaving and finishing machinery," he said, "but through every department and every building and into every basement and attic." When he took the trip, seven days were needed to complete it. The extensive inspection would have taken longer had it not been possible to pass from mill to mill by covered bridges.

With the completion of the large new dam and power plant in 1923, Amoskeag had the greatest waterpower of any textile mill in the country. The new hydroelectric development reduced the company's power costs to the lowest possible point, a very important factor due to the increasing problems in connection with the supply and price of coal. During the first six months of operation, when a maximum of 35,734 horse power was produced, up to 23,316 of the amount was generated at the new power plant. The balance was made by old wheels in the canals. Amoskeag had 34 water wheels. The company had another great waterpower site which could be developed at some future date to furnish an additional 15,000 to 20,000 horsepower, if the coal situation should become more difficult. In addition to the power supplied by water, Amoskeag power equipment also included three huge steam plants with 219 boilers.

The fact that the un-utilized waterpower site would remain so unless the current coal situation should worsen was reflective of the increasing superiority of coal as an energy source. The Merrimack River, the one geographical advantage which resulted in textiles first being produced in New England, was no longer the only economical energy source. At this point new mill locations were independent of waterpower.

The number of employees at Amoskeag averaged 13,500 a week in the prewar period. Of course, during 1922 while the nearly 10 months' strike lasted, the weekly average was very low. The average employed in 1923 was 10,322. The next year there was an increase to 11,998.

The number of employees on the payroll in 1925 was 15,000, including 8,250 men and 6,750 women. The amount paid out in wages that year was $16.2 million. Amoskeag had distributed a total of $261 million in wages from 1831 to 1925.

Demands of workers at Amoskeag increased following the postwar boom and the 1922 strike. In April, 1923, Amoskeag increased wages 12 1/2 percent, which was similar to other mills in New England. It was in that year the company arranged a plan to give employees representation. The initial meeting was held May 31, 1923. Amoskeag's chief competitor, Riverside & Dan River Cotton Mills in Virginia, had organized an employee representation plan called an industrial democracy. The plan at Amoskeag was under the direction of William Swallow, the company's employment manager. Agent W. Parker Straw had sent him to visit the Western Electric Co. to see how its successful employee representation system was organized and operated. Treasurer F. C. Dumaine was very interested in the Amoskeag plan and attended the annual banquets of the organization.

The plan itself was prepared by a committee of employee representatives of different crafts, in joint session with representatives of management. Its purpose was to give employees a voice in regard to conditions under which they worked, and to provide an orderly and expeditious procedure for the prevention and adjustment of differences. There were joint departmental committees to which the management appointed overseers, second-hands, and salaried officials. Joint sectional committees and a general joint committee completed the organization. The departments represented were cotton-carding, spinning, dressing, weaving, cloth finishing; worsted-preparing, spinning, weaving, finishing; machine shop and foundry; and the electrical, steam and waterpower; construction and maintenance; and transportation.

The cotton section at Amoskeag was in a depressed condition in 1923, especially in the latter part of the year. The worsted department at the same time operated at a fairly high and even rate. On October 4, 1923, the company announced that all mills except the worsted department would close for an indefinite period. This was the first indefinite shutdown since 1893. The notice to employees read:

> Conditions in business necessitate an immediate curtailment in
> our cotton department at this time. Accordingly this department
> will be closed Saturday noon, October 6, for an indefinite pe-
> riod. As business improves and we are able to start various looms,
> notice will appear in the newspapers. The worsted and chemical
> departments will not be affected and will run as usual.

The cause of the shutdown was the continuing decline in the demand for ginghams. This was in spite of the fact quotations were at
the same level as in the preceding year, although cotton was 5 cents
a pound and wages 15 percent higher than in 1922. Failure of buyers
to respond had resulted in operations at the mills being reduced to
four days a week at 75 percent capacity.

Amoskeag management had always opposed the accumulation of
goods and it was generally understood that the cotton department
would not reopen until there were plenty of orders booked. The
worsted department would remain busy. This was not a big proposition, however, because it had only 60,000 spindles. Approximately
10,000 hands were idle due to the suspension of operations in the
cotton department.

Agent Straw, who had conferred with the overseers and representatives of employees before announcing the closing of the mills, said
that management was hopeful of a change in conditions and alluded
to the possibility of developing business in lines other than staple
goods, which were then moving slowly. Although the outlook was
unfavorable for ginghams and flannel, Agent Straw did not want the
employees or the public to get a feeling of extreme pessimism.

In the fall of 1924, Agent W. Parker Straw discussed with employee representatives the idea of the employees taking a 20 percent
reduction in wages to stimulate business and allow the company to
compete with other mills in other sections of the country. A joint
convention of employee representatives, on September 16, unanimously rejected the proposal. Some said they were willing to accept a
smaller cut. The convention finally voted to take a 5 percent cut.
Agent Straw's counter proposal that they accept 15 percent was rejected. He said that 5 percent would be useless. It meant less than a
third of a cent per yard of cloth. He reiterated that 20 percent was

necessary to get the best results in the market, offering that it was not advisable to produce goods for future orders. He then said he would accept the employees' next offer as final. At the end of October, it was voted to agree to a 10 percent cut, but the reduction was not put into effect immediately.

When the company opened its lines it was unable to reduce prices because of the rise in the price of cotton. Mr. Straw explained that he wanted to be fair and square with the workers and told them that less than 1,000 cases had been sold. He said that competitors got business because of their lower prices. There had been cancellations since the opening and the company did not have a single order on hand. He said that under such conditions 10 percent would be of no use, as the company would not be able to sell another yard of cloth at the prices recently quoted. He also stated that management did not want to cut wages, but it must to get the business. To break even, the expenses of the company would have to be reduced 33 1/3 percent. According to Mr. Straw, the company was willing to absorb part of this amount, and, if a 20 percent cut had been accepted the mills would then have been in full operation. Workers again offered to take a 10 percent reduction until April 1925. Agent Straw finally accepted the decision of the convention, but said he did so "with expression of sorrow" for the action taken.

A week before April 1, 1925, when the above agreement was to expire, employees met to hear the recommendations of Agent Straw. He told them that unless they wished to stop things immediately and bring disaster to present activity, it would be necessary to keep wages at the present level for the next six months. He added that he thought Manchester's condition was better than in many places and hoped that better and busier times were coming. The convention agreed to continue the cut for another three months. However, Agent Straw said it would require that much time just to get orders, manufacture and deliver them. Six months would be a short enough period, but nine months would be better. The convention then agreed to a continuation of the wage cut for six months. But better conditions and business were slow to come.

The continued heavy operating losses suffered by Amoskeag in these years showed clearly that the company was in a period of declining activity. The unsatisfactory situation was referred to by Treasurer Dumaine in his report at the annual meeting held on October 20, 1924. Here is his complete statement to stockholders:

This report is one of the poorest, if not the poorest, ever presented for your consideration, and I am sorry indeed that it falls to my lot to present it to you.

These figures show that the period under discussion offers an excellent illustration of the restrictive effect of high prices of cotton and the high cost of manufacturing combined.

During the past year there has never been a time when it was possible to purchase cotton, convert it into finished goods and dispose of them on a basis yielding the slightest profit.

This condition has also prevailed in the worsted department.

The most unfortunate part of it is that I am unable to tell you at the moment anything which might encourage you as to any improvement in conditions in the immediate future.

It would seem that so extended a period of unprofitable business must sooner or later end. The management, however, sees no such possibility at present and would be satisfied if the mills could be run fairly full and pay a reasonable wage without a destructive loss.

Every known economy consistent with safety and proper care of property has been instituted and all unnecessary work discontinued.

Fortunately, in the better years gone by, a reasonable surplus had been retained for just such times as these which enables us to maintain a proper upkeep and has justified the board making a decision which otherwise would not have been possible.

The management greatly regrets the necessity of the drastic curtailment of operation, and the impossibility of continuing employment for the greater number of loyal people who for a long period have worked in the mills, but it has been impossible to Dispose of the output, and curtailment has therefore been compulsory.

The relations between the company and the employees are amicable and there is a tendency to cooperate and trust each other. It is desirable that these relations continue. Upon the success of the venture depends the welfare of both the employees and the company.

Since last year's meeting, the new dam and power station have been completed and placed in operation. During the first six months of the year an average of 23,596 horsepower, based on 54 hours weekly, was developed from water alone. The maximum amount during the period was 35,734 and the minimum 7,671 horsepower. Of this total the new power station produced an average of 15,650 with a maximum of 23,316 and a minimum of 6,331 horsepower. The balance was made by old wheels in the canals.

During the spring, and frequently in the fall, great quantities of water pass over the dam which it is impossible to utilize [for waterpower].

In connection with others located upon the Merrimack, flowage rights have been acquired and a new dam built at Merrymount Pond, in New Durham, which will tend to help maintain a more even flow in the river.

Some general scheme should be devised and eventually carried out by which the water during freshest periods can be stored back in the country and used in the drought of summer months.

The advancing cost of fuel for steam makes it imperative to take advantage of this, as well as all other, opportunities for savings if New England is to continue operations against the infinitely lower cost of manufacturing in other parts of the country.

My whole life has been spent in the service of this great New Hampshire industry and my keen interest in its property constrains me to point out to the citizens of this State the danger of so changing the laws as to make it harder to continue manufacturing. Many New Hampshire people have substantial investment in her industries and the livelihood of a large part of the people directly depends upon the operation of these industries. To restrict further the hours of labor will endanger both.

Many workers fear the effect upon their welfare should the hours of operation be reduced, for it is as sure as night follows day, that the same wage could not be paid for a shorter day. Moreover, it is evident that shorter hours will postpone the time when the mills can give full employment. Our product must compete with goods made in other states which permit longer hours. The time will come when it will be possible for us to make goods at a profit and it will come sooner with a 54-hour week than with a shorter one. We do not enjoy any vital advantage over other sections of the country. If artificial restrictions, from which these sections are free, should be increased, we can't expect to compete with them. New Hampshire needs legislation based upon the theory of common sense, enacted with care and thought, and for the good of the greater number.

The results of the post-strike profitability are demonstrated below.

Amoskeag Profitability
For Fiscal Years 1907-1925

	Company Totals in 1,000s			*Per Share Adjusted for Splits*		
Year	Earnings	Dividends	Surplus	Earnings	Dividends	Surplus
1907	$1,232	$922	$310	$21.39	$16.00	$5.59
1908	1,251	922	329	21.72	16.00	5.72
1909	782	691	91	13.58	12.00	1.58
1910	761	691	70	13.21	12.00	1.21
1911	722	691	31	12.53	12.00	.53
1912	1,104	1,037	67	19.17	18.00	1.17
1913	1,063	1,037	26	18.44	18.00	.44
1914	1,023	1,037	(14)	17.76	18.00	(.24)
1915	1,079	1,037	42	18.73	18.00	.73
1916	1,179	1,037	142	20.47	18.00	2.47
1917	1,334	1,037	297	23.16	18.00	5.16
1918	5,053	1,037	4,016	87.72	18.00	69.72
1919	7,945	1,167	6,778	137.93	20.24	117.69
1920	4,369	1,685	2,684	75.85	29.25	46.60
1921	1,273	2,524	(1,251)	22.10	43.82	(21.72)
1922	648	2,524	(1,876)	11.25	43.82	(32.57)
1923	(75)	2,005	(2,080)	(1.30)	34.81	(36.11)
1924	(2,851)	1,487	(4,338)	(49.50)	25.81	(75.31)
1925	(456)	709	(1,165)	(7.92)	12.31	(20.23)

This chart is an expansion of the one presented in the previous chapter. The company's performance in 1922 and 1923 are not as significant an indication of its long-term earning potential, since both year's performances were hurt by the nine-month strike. However, in years ending in 1924 and 1925, Amoskeag had combined losses in excess of $3.3 million. It was no longer a matter of cutting dividends to prevent a loss in surplus. Unless Dumaine could attain the wage parody with the South that was sought in 1922, manufacturing in Manchester could not be conducted on a profitable basis.

Toward the end of 1924, Dumaine made the following entry in his diary, reflecting his concern for the ability of Amoskeag to operate profitably in the future.

Saturday, November 15, 1924:

*The outlook for textiles in New England is, to my mind, most uncertain and to such an extent that, feeling as I do today, should a reasonable bona fide offer be made for the [Amoskeag] property, I am sure I would recommend its sale. Failing in securing an offer, were the property mine, I do not doubt I would cease operations and wreck the concern of what it would bring for junk, **were it not for the sentiment I have and feeling perhaps it would disappoint the men who brought me up and managed the company so many previous years.** I am sure we could   liquidate, junk the mills and give the shareholders a sum of money, which, if conservatively invested, would undoubtedly yield a greater amount of money than they could possibly receive on Amoskeag stock.*

I am writing this statement this particular day and shall be interested in ten or twenty years to know how the result compares with today's outlook.

During the post-strike years it was frequently emphasized in the investment market that Amoskeag stock was really far below the current asset values. On one instance when the preferred was selling at $75 and the common at $51 for a combined market value of $24.5 million, the company had a current asset value of $43.7 million, representing a discount of over $19 million. This meant that Amoskeag's current assets were selling in the open market for 57 cents on the dollar, before assigning any value to the mills and hydroelectric plant.

The fact that the stock price, evaluated on a future earnings bases, was less than 50 percent of the liquidation value when any reasonable amount was assigned to the plant, meant that the company was worth twice as much dead as alive. Current stockholders were becoming increasingly uncomfortable with the outlook of continual losses eroding away past accumulated earnings. It was only a matter of time before outside interests attracted by this extreme spread between the stock's market price and its breakup value would look upon Amoskeag as a takeover target with the ultimate objective of liquidating this once great textile firm.

It was to this issue that Dumaine next turned his attention.

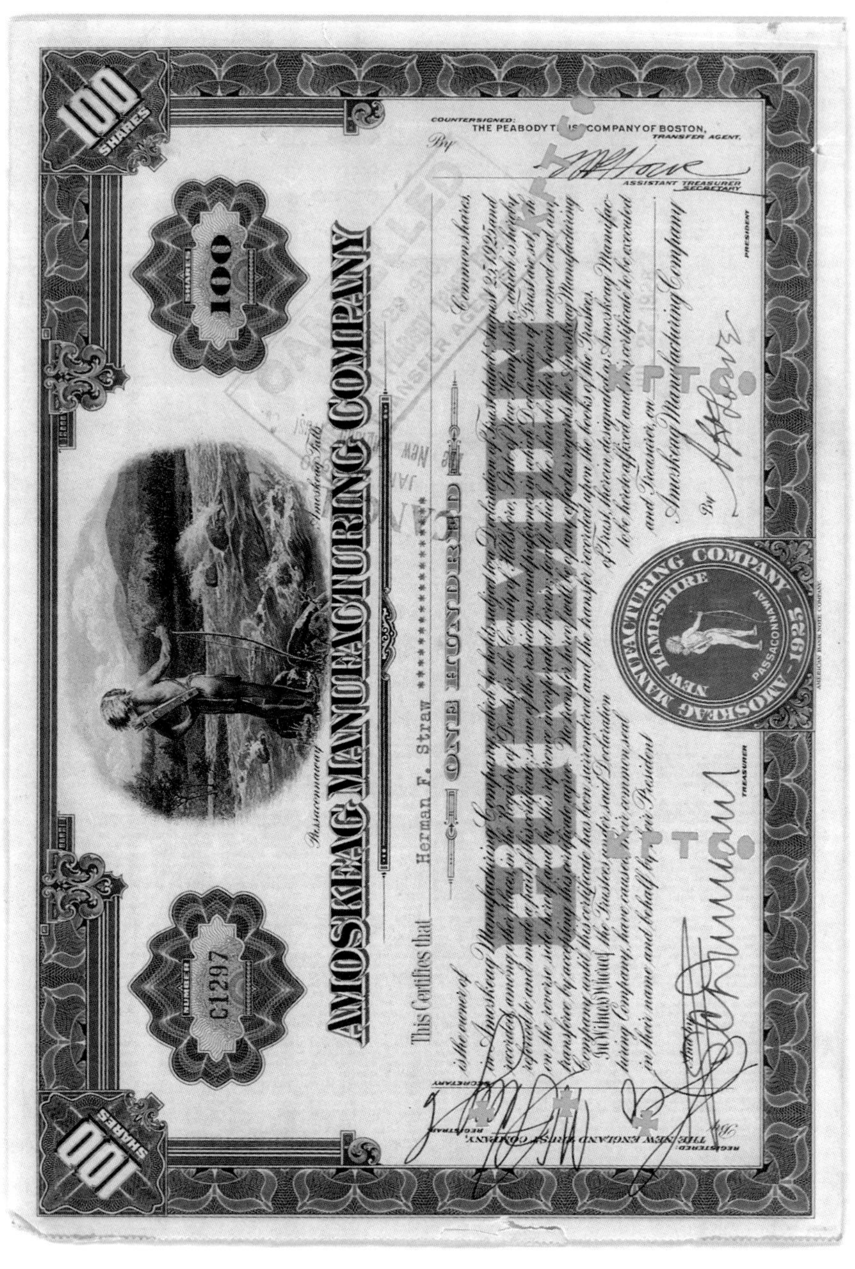

CHAPTER VII

Corporate Restructuring

Based on Dumaine's October 20, 1924, report as printed in the previous chapter, the trustees announced that the common dividend due the following month would not be approved. They explained that this action was made necessary by "uncontrollable conditions in the textile business." They "trusted that the owners will agree that the preservation of the property and the maintenance of its resources is of greater importance." No further payments were made on the common stock, and dividends on the preferred were discontinued after February 2, 1926. Prior to this action, Amoskeag had an uninterrupted dividend record that began in 1834.

In an effort to offset declining demand for gingham, Amoskeag was experimenting with the production of rayon cloth. Three new lines of rayon mixtures were offered in 1925 as Rayon Rayonelle, San Ray and Cherry Blossom Rayon. They were all 38-inch fabrics and were said to be "superior to most rayon offerings because of their firm construction, guaranteed fast colors and a wide range of patterns and style content." It was also stated that they included dolby, printed yarn, striped and plaid effects, novelty yarns, lace and overplaid work, two- and three-tone effects, honeycomb and granite weaves and wide and narrow sport stripes, and all imaginable color arrangements. The finish of these popular-priced cotton and rayon dress materials were said to be "soft and the fabrics had more suppleness than most of such goods on the market, which were made from a different character of rayon than most lines."

The new fabrics were highly endorsed by New York buyers, and Boston people who had examined some of the "rayonized" cotton samples, declared they were "the most beautiful they had ever seen."

Following this fine reception of Amoskeag lines, it became known in the market that the company's Manchester plant, for the manufacture of its own rayon requirements, was nearing completion and was expected to be in production in a short time.

When the new rayon lines were offered in the early fall of 1925, it was said that they would supplement two lines of highly styled novelties and ginghams. In a meeting of employee representatives held September 25, 1925, Agent W. Parker Straw made it clear that to meet the company's problems it was necessary to shift production from high grade staples, particularly ginghams, which had been Amoskeag's mainstay, to the manufacture of styled fabrics. "Staple ginghams, as far as we are concerned, are hopeless," he said. "What we are interested in is diversification, including the manufacture of fancy goods such as striped flannels and rayons."

The rayon yarn unit began operation in 1926. In the March 26 issue of the "Manchester Leader," it was reported that after two and a half years of experimenting, Amoskeag's rayon plant had just been put into operation and the company was now ready to supply 2,000 looms with its own rayon. Agent Straw was enthusiastic about the outlook for Amoskeag in the new field. However, as Treasurer Dumaine said in his 1925-1926 report, the rayon unit was "a comparatively small affair" with only enough production for the company's own needs in fancy goods. In his opinion, it wasn't advisable to increase production beyond that point. After a few months of operation, the company reported that "the rayon department was doing remarkably well and was producing a much higher grade of rayon than was expected for the time it had been in operation."

Some of the rayon was sold to other mills. Buyers included Royal Little and the Suncook Mills. The Amoskeag Company wove some shirtings from its own rayon and made other men's wear fabrics. In later years, a large part of its rayon cloth production was taffetas for mufflers.

There were different opinions as to the reasons for the discontinuance of the rayon yarn plant in 1933. Some critics said production was hampered by lack of adequate equipment. There was a feeling that enough money had not been put into the project to make it continuously successful. The initial investment of $121,000 was insufficient. Another $164,000 was added in 1926. The plant showed small losses, after depreciation, until 1927, when the first profit was $129,000. In the following year, another $184,000 was put into the project. Production reached a total of about 20,000 pounds a week, or around 1,000,000 pounds annually.

Labor problems was another explanation for closing of the rayon unit. To keep the spinnerets operational, the plant had to be operated 24 hours a day, seven days a week, but problems ensued due to a continuous challenge of getting women who were willing to fit into such a schedule. After seven years of operation, the company decided to end making its own rayon yarns. With the realization that labor costs could not be lowered there was no reason to expand investment in rayon machinery.

About the same time, the gingham market was shrinking. One suggestion to shore it up was volume production of sheets and blankets. There were 1,000 looms on sheetings, including Langdon bleached 76s and GBs. At one point, it appeared as though the company's entrance into the sheet and pillow case business might be realized. Undoubtedly there were a number of reasons for the decision to not make sheets. Not much was done with blankets either, despite the fact that they had all the equipment needed to make them, except the looms. There was a tremendous napping department on the west side of the river and a set of Davis & Furber 3-cylinder woolen cards in the worsted plant. Some sample part-cotton blankets were manufactured, but because the needed looms were not purchased, commercial production was not possible.

The author's opinion is that the primary reason for deciding not to expand production into these alternative fields was the fact that those New England firms producing blankets and sheeting were at a similar cost disadvantage as was Amoskeag in gingham. It would not be prudent to make a substantial investment in new machines when the firm knew it could not produce at a cost competitive with the Southern mills. As with the decision on the discontinuation of rayon, it was one thing to make minor capital replacement investments with an aim to keep production as cost efficient as possible. It was an altogether different decision to embark on a major capital investment when the outcome would obviously be production at a loss.

At the same time that Amoskeag was experimenting with alternative product lines, it was investigating the possibility of altering its financial structure to ease stockholders concern. They were becoming increasingly distressed that accumulated earnings from past production would be squandered away through continual production at a loss. On August 7, 1925, the trustees unanimously approved a plan for the formation of a new trust, which would take over all of the company's fixed assets, inventories and accounts receivable, together with the fixed assets associated with the acquisition of the Parkhill Manufacturing of Fitchburg, Massachusetts. The plan was explained in a letter to shareholders who were asked to attend a meeting August 25 to act on the proposal. The new trust would carry the old title "Amoskeag Manufacturing Company," which would own and operate the plant facilities at Manchester and Fitchburg. In addition to receivables and inventories, its current assets would include $6 million in cash.

The existing trust would be renamed Amoskeag Company and, as a legal continuation of the original 1831 corporation, would retain all cash above the $6 million mentioned and all investments in securities. In this manner the Amoskeag stockholders would have their retained earnings beyond the $6 million amount protected from being used for subsidizing the current unprofitable operation. At the same time, Amoskeag Company would be a holding company of the new Amoskeag Manufacturing Company. This could be to the advantage of the stockholders if the manufacturing company were to become profitable in the future. Unfortunately, conditions in the New England cotton industry never significantly improved.

The new trust would have an authorized capital of 285,000 shares of six percent preferred and 365,000 common shares, both of no par value. Dividends on the preferred would be cumulative after January 1, 1929. The mills machinery, land, and water power of the Amoskeag and Parkhill would be paid for in stock of the new company on the basis of appraised value. The new company's preferred would be distributed to Amoskeag and Parkhill on the basis of net working capital.

Details of this arrangement when worked out would result in the Amoskeag Company, or holding company, 264,720 shares of preferred for $26.7 million of current assets, and receiving 330,000 shares

Nos. 7 and 8 Mills

of new common for $14.5 million of fixed assets or a total of $41.2 million. These shares represented 92 and 90 percent, respectively, of each kind of stock in the operating company. The remaining stock went to the former owners of the Parkhill Manufacturing Company. The trustees decided to acquire the Fitchburg mills at this time to increase Amoskeag's share of textile production in New England. In fact, one reason for leaving $6 million in cash, which was far in excess of cash necessary for operation, was to have a ready source of money to purchase other mills in New England if they could be acquired at an attractive price. The other obvious reason for the $6 million balance was to provide the operating corporation with funds until it could be operated profitably on its own.

The cash and investment securities the holding company retained were valued at $18.7 million. In a letter to shareholders, the trustees said that the organization of a separate operating company and the consolidation of the Amoskeag and Parkhill would be advantageous. Shareholders were advised to approve and authorize the sale.

Parkhill was well known to the trade and for a number of years had been regarded as a successfully managed gingham mill. Arthur H. Lowe, treasurer of the Parkhill, was one of the most active, forward looking men in the cotton industry and it was the general opinion that, in the consolidation with the Amoskeag, his judgement and activity would be depended on to a large extent. His son, Russell B. Lowe, Parkhill president, was being counted on to make his contribution to the management of the newly enlarged Amoskeag Manufacturing Company.

At the August 24 special meeting, the Parkhill merger and the proposed plan of recapitalization were approved. Eighty-five shareholders were at the meeting, the largest attendance in years. F.P. Carpenter of Manchester, a trustee for many years, presided and B.E. Eames, counsel for the company, presented the vote for approval. But there was some opposition from one of the Manchester stockholders. Lawrence J. Harrington declared that the shareholders had not received enough information about the plan to cast an intelligent vote. He presented a resolution with a list of questions for management to answer before stockholders' approval of the plan should be definitely asked. Attention was called to the losses of the past three years and to the fact that manufacturing operations were operating at only 60 percent of capacity and that Southern competition was becoming more serious. Mr. Harrington's questions about the Parkhill business pertained to whether it had been losing money and whether Amoskeag trustees owned shares in that company. The resolution asked that questions about both mills be answered prior to taking the vote for the proposal.

Dumaine declared that by acquiring Parkhill, Amoskeag would get the benefit of its organization and cotton mills, some new talent and valuable younger men. Parkhill's goods could be marketed through Amoskeag's own organization. This merger would give the company the nucleus of a manufacturing organization in the South and enable it to check up on the relative costs and taxes in New England and the South. He stated that the Parkhill Mills had been running night and day. So far as he knew, the only common ownership of shares was 100 shares of common and 100 shares of preferred of Amoskeag owned by Treasurer A. H. Lowe. The Parkhill stock was all owned by the Lowe's, their family and a few friends, he added.

The Harrington resolution was defeated by a vote of 357,000 to 5,000, following a rather complete statement by Dumaine about the Amoskeag condition and the purpose and expected advantages from the merger and the setting up of a new operating company. When put to vote, the complete plan, including the proposed change in the name of the old company to Amoskeag Company, was approved by the stockholders.

Responding to a question on hours of labor and criticism of his management of the company during the strike, Dumaine explained that mills could not be run successfully in New Hampshire unless they were operating under the same conditions as mills in other parts of the country competing for the same market. He pointed out that Manchester taxes were more than double those in the South.

As for segregation of invested funds, the treasurer explained that with such an arrangement there would no longer be any danger of stockholders losing these funds in business. In the future, what money Amoskeag would make or lose would be from manufacturing operations alone. The segregated funds would always remain, no longer subject to business vicissitudes. Harrington had asked why segregated funds should not be distributed to stockholders, who were receiving no income. Dumaine explained that it was an issue in the hands of the trustees. Although there was no objection to such a distribution, he said he personally would prefer to have the funds remain in the organization to be invested in Treasury notes and corporate securities for the benefit of stockholders.

The immediate effect of the reorganization on Amoskeag common stock prices was significant. In April 1925 it had been quoted at $61.50. Later there was an advance to the lower $70. On August 6, the day before the trustees approved the reorganization plan, the trade already knew about it and the expectation of some kind of a cash distribution with the formation of the new company boosted the price of Amoskeag common on the Boston Stock Exchange from $72 to $92, an advance of 20 points in only 20 minutes. The drop in price to $76 the following week evidently reflected the speculative disappointment over the failure of the trustees to take action toward resumption of common dividends or the distribution of some portion of the segregated investments amounting to $18.7 million, or $52 a share on the 345,600 shares of common.

The manufacturing properties were conveyed to the new operating company through six trustees who held office only for one day, August 25, and immediately were replaced by a permanent board of nine elected members: Charles F. Adams, Philip Dexter, F. C. Dumaine, F. C. Dumaine, Jr., William C. Endicott, George P. Gardner, Arthur H. Lowe, Russell B. Lowe, and George Wigglesworth. Five of these trustees were also on the board of the old trust, which was continued as a holding company with the new title of the Amoskeag Company. They were Messrs. Adams, Dexter, Dumaine, Sr., Gardner and Wigglesworth. Dumaine served as treasurer of both companies. One of the new members, Arthur H. Lowe, who had been treasurer of Parkhill, was elected president of the new Amoskeag Manufacturing Company. Wigglesworth continued as president of the old company. Herman F. Straw, former agent, continued as secretary. On September 1, the selling of the Parkhill products, formerly merchandised through Amory, Browne & Co., was taken over by Amoskeag's own selling agency, Jarvis, Loomis & Dunbar.

Of particular interest was the reference to Parkhill's small spinning mill at West Helena, Arkansas, and Dumaine's statement that it would give Amoskeag the nucleus of a manufacturing organization in the South to enable the management to examine relative costs and taxes in that part of the country. Over several years, Dumaine had kept in touch with developments in the South, and he and Agent Herman F. Straw had made at least one trip to obtain firsthand information on labor conditions and wages. But it was always the policy of the Amoskeag management to continue in New Hampshire as long as possible. About 1914, the company had an opportunity to purchase the four mills in Columbia, South Carolina, later taken over by the Pacific. It was decided not to accept the offer on the basis that Amoskeag was a New England institution, the stockholders and management were New England people, an intractable policy of long standing.

The financial results of the reorganization are shown in the balance sheets of the Amoskeag Manufacturing Company and Amoskeag Company as of October 28 and October 1, 1925.

Inventories recorded some $10 million higher than previously recorded. The vast majority of the increase is likely to be a result of appraising current assets at an amount closer to their real values and thus discontinuing Amoskeag's policy of underestimating assets on the balance sheet.

At the October 28, 1925, annual meeting, Dumaine reviewed the past 20 years during when he was treasurer of Amoskeag. He pointed out that the results attained had not been based on the policy of distributing all earnings but by applying a reasonable part of them in good years to improvement of property and the accumulation of reserves for bad years. He added that he did not know of any mill which had so conclusively demonstrated the soundness of its methods, and hoped that the next 20 years would show results as good through consistent application of the principles which had put the company in a position "to ride out the worst storm the textile industry had known in that century."

The trial balance of the Amoskeag Company prior to the separation of the manufacturing company as of June 1, 1925, showed total financial assets of $18,686,707, including $59,658 in cash, $17,138,000 of Fourth Liberty Loan Bonds and $1,489,049 in miscellaneous investments. The balance sheets of October 28, 1925 and May 29, 1926 compare as follows:

AMOSKEAG MANUFACTURING COMPANY
Comparative Balance Sheet

	Oct. 28, 1925	June 30, 1926	Dec. 31, 1926
	Assets		
Plant	$16,695,843	$16,686,227	$16,648,576
	Current Assets		
Cash	1,556,998	1,704,571	3,815,071
Liberty Bond	4,448,500	4,448,500	4,448,500
Accounts Receivable	6,939,125	7,192,080	5,392,150
Cotton Inventory	9,079,788	6,437,221	4,742,165
Wool Inventory	4,970,897	4,535,353	4,299,441
Mfg. Supplies	1,474,015	642,056	522,688
Miscellaneous	24,081	302,232	558,974
Total Current Assets	$28,503,404	$25,262,014	$23,814,989
Total Assets	$45,199,247	$41,948,241	$40,463,565
	Liabilities		
Accts. and Notes Payable		$ 1,000,116	$ 38,249
Reserves for Shareholders	$45,199,247	$40,948,009	$40,425,316
Total Liabilities & Equity	$45,199,247	$41,948,125	$40,463,565
Net Current	$28,503,404	$24,261,898	$23,740,740

Amoskeag Company's capital consisted of 100,000 shares of $4.50 preferred and 345,600 shares of common, the stock of the original trust which it continued. The shares of Amoskeag Company stocks listed in the balance sheet below represents treasury stock. The holding company also owned 264,720 shares of 6 percent preferred and 330,000 shares of common of the new operating Amoskeag Manufacturing Company in addition to the listed investments. Since the earning capacity of the manufacturing company was questionable these holdings were not included in the holding company's balance sheet presentation.

The net effect of this reorganization was that the old trust, now called Amoskeag Company turned over all of its mills, inventories, and receivables, together with $6 million in cash and government securities, in exchange for more than 90 percent of the stock of the new trust, which retained the name Amoskeag Manufacturing Company The remaining stock went to the principals of Parkhill in exchange for their plant and current assets. In the process the Amoskeag Company withdrew the remaining $18 million in government bonds and other investments from the manufacturing company.

AMOSKEAG COMPANY
Comparative Balance Sheets

Assets	October 28, 1925	May 29, 1926
Cash	$ 54,312	$ 45,211
4th Liberty Loan Bonds	24,251,500	24,369,800
Amoskeag Company pfd (6,157 shares)	464,854	461,775
Amoskeag Company com (3,284 shares)	233,164	180,620
Miscellaneous Investments	820,892	748,754
Total Market Value	$ 25,824,722	$ 25,806,160
Deduct Notes Payable	$ 7,295,000	$ 6,500,000
Equity	$ 18,529,722	$ 19,306,160

Amoskeag Company's first income statement as a holding company is below. The income from investments was over $750,000. In prior years, the income from investments must have approached $1 million, since there was the additional $6 million left in the manufacturing company. If one were to try to measure the basic income from manufacturing for the years since the war, then it would be prudent to reduce income by approximately $1 million a year.

A comparison of the cash and security balances of the manufacturing company following the formation of the new trust with the bal-

---

AMOSKEAG COMPANY
INCOME ACCOUNT FOR YEAR ENDED MAY 29, 1926

Interest and Dividend Income	$1,092,248
Interest charges	319,104
Other deductions	14,346
Net Income	$ 758,798
Preferred Dividends	450,000
Earning Available for Common Stock	$ 308,798

---

ances that existed prior to the high profits generated in the war years indicates that the $6 million left in the new trust represented excess working capital. These funds could be used to offset future poor performances or to provide the manufacturing company with a ready cash fund with which to acquire other New England textile firms such as Parkhill if they became available at a reasonable price. This latter possibility was mentioned by Dumaine in the 1936 bankruptcy hearings. No evaluation as to the possibility of excess receivables and inventories left with the manufacturing company can be made because the amount of understatement of these accounts in the prewar years cannot be determined.

Because the old trust owned more than 90 percent of the stock of the new trust, with the remaining percentage held by a few Parkhill interests, the stock of the new trust was not listed on the exchange. The old trust, the Amoskeag Company, however, continued to be traded on the Boston Stock Exchange.

Following the bankruptcy of the manufacturing company in 1936, Amoskeag directors in general and Dumaine in particular were criticized for the corporate reorganization by many who believed it was the first step in a planned liquidation. It was further alleged that Amoskeag directors had no concern for the employees or the city.

Another interpretation of the 1925 reorganization is that Dumaine and the other Amoskeag directors were trying to balance their responsibilities to their employees with their fiduciary obligations to their stockholders.

The separation of the manufacturing assets from the holding company was a way of telling the increasing number of dissatisfied stockholders that the vast majority of their surplus would not be squandered on a losing proposition. On the other hand, because Amoskeag owned more than 90 percent of the manufacturing company, it was in a position to provide the manufacturing company with additional funds were such a move to become financially advantageous.

As for its obligations to employees and the city, it was important that the company left an extra $6 million in the operating company to give it every opportunity to survive.

By July 1927, Amoskeag common shares were down to $48.50, the lowest in many years. No dividends were being paid on either common or preferred. Previous average quotations on Amoskeag common were $92 in 1921, $112 in 1922, $89 in 1923, $70 in 1924, $76 in 1925 and $59 in 1926.

In August, the trustees of the Amoskeag Company were informed through Curtis, Sanger & Co., investment bankers, that certain New York interests wanted to purchase the holding company to liquidate assets at a price substantially larger than current quoted market prices for its stock. The prime mover was Edward C. Carrington, who asked for a 60-day option for the purchase of Amoskeag shares at $100 and accrued dividends for the preferred and $90 for the common, which was quoted at near $60, plus additional money after the liquidation of the current assets, payment of expenses and brokers' commissions. Such a change in ownership of the holding company, which controlled more than 90 percent of the stock of the manufacturing trust, was expected to result in the liquidation of the latter's properties.

Some suspected that Carrington might be representing E.I. Dupont De Nemours & Co., which could develop the Amoskeag plants into a rayon manufacturing organization.

Another possible interest was New England Power Co. of Northern New Hampshire who wanted the Amoskeag hydroelectric plant and other water power developments to connect its northern and southern New Hampshire fields. No matter, for what was important was that attention was called to the offering price for the holding company, involving control of practically all of the stock of the manufacturing organization, which was not equal to the worth of the combined current assets. The point was that any buyer would get the fixed assets for nothing.

The option sought by the New York interests was refused by the trustees of the holding company at a meeting held September 8, but they decided to put the matter of liquidation up to the shareholders at the annual meeting on October 5. Prior to the October meeting they informed the shareholders of the offer and of the trustees' response. At the October meeting, by a vote of 356,803 to 955, the trustees were authorized:

> . . . if they deem it wise, to liquidate in their discretion, the whole, or any part, of the assets of your company, upon such terms and conditions as they deem for the best interests of the shareholders.

The shares present or represented by proxy included 75,016 preferred and 286,056 common, 80.55 and 83.5 percent of the outstanding stock, which was assuredly more than the required two-thirds. A motion by Garrard Glenn, representative of Carrington, asked trustees to investigate any offer they might receive for the property and report to the stockholders, and also that the meeting be adjourned for two weeks for that purpose. Because it had not been published in the call, the motion was ruled out of order.

The trustees' reasons for rejecting the New York offer, Dumaine explained, was that it had been 96 years since the original charter was granted to Amoskeag. During that whole time, the company had continued to grow and prosper. There had been good times and bad

Main mills from the river

times, though perhaps not quite as bad as in that period and the preceding three or four years. Bills and obligations of every sort had always been paid and the return to owners compared favorably with those of other New England textile companies. The owners had never required the shareholders to help finance the company out of their own pockets. Amoskeag had always had good management, quite competent to manage its own affairs without the volunteer assistance of outsiders. Management felt no need for any outsider to tell them when or how to liquidate the company. There was no intention of abandoning operations in Manchester or to subject the city to the devastation that they knew such a move would produce. Ties of interest and sentiment would continue to bind them to the city and the community. Dumaine concluded that with the assistance of the shareholders, the employees and with the community's support, the company would prefer to remain in business if it were possible without loss of assets. Failing in that, the trustees would presumably liquidate in an orderly manner, in accordance with the authority just granted to them by the shareholders.

After the meeting, however, many people said they believed the stage was set for Amoskeag's gradual withdrawal from the Queen City.

The importance of Amoskeag to Manchester was continually emphasized and discussed. The company and its welfare were the heart beat of the city. Practically half of Manchester's 84,000 population depended entirely on the mills for support. Nearly 50 percent of the other half were indirectly dependent on Amoskeag. Many believed the mills would continue in some way, ridiculing the idea that the plant would be junked. Attention was called to the fact that gradual liquidation was already in process, as demonstrated by the company's disposal in recent months of thousands of dollars worth of property, both land and buildings.

Above all, the general opinion was that Amoskeag was fully capable of doing its own liquidation if such a development were decided.

A second significant change in the Amoskeag financial situation took place in November. A new recapitalization plan went into effect, regarded by many as the second phase leading to the final liquidation of the manufacturing company. By the middle of November rumors were rampant of a proposed plan for the manufacturing company to repurchase the 93.37 percent of its 6 percent preferred owned to retire them and all other stock and replace the preferred stock with a bond issue. The expectation that this would lead to a substantial distribution by the Amoskeag Company resulted in an advance of 9 1/4 points in the market value of the latter's common stock in one day, bringing it up to $99.25. On the afternoon of November 21, the day set by the trustees for special meetings with the stockholders of both companies to consider the proposed purchase, the common stock of the holding company was quoted at 103 to 108.

Three meetings were held. At the first meeting on the morning of November 21, Dumaine, who was serving double duty as trustee and treasurer of both trusts, recommended that the operating trust retire its whole issue of 285,000 shares of preferred stock held by Amoskeag Company and Parkhill interests for $8.1 million in cash, plus $14.7 million in new 20-year, 6 percent bonds, and 13,191 additional common shares. The trustees, subject to the approval of the shareholders, unanimously adopted resolutions to amend the declaration of trust, to repurchase the preferred stock, issue the bonds and additional common stock, and list the shares of the trust on the Boston Stock Exchange.

At the second meeting at noon, a certified copy of all three resolutions, with full detail, was presented to the shareholders of the operating trust in Manchester. By affirmative vote of every share of both preferred and common stock these resolutions were "in all respects approved, ratified and confirmed." Attention was called to the fact that whereas the bond interest requirement would be $879,900 annually, the payments of dividends on the 6 percent preferred, which were to become cumulative in 1929, would have been $1,710,000 a year. This would place the manufacturing company's common in a correspondingly better position. There would then be 378,191 shares of the latter outstanding, compared to 365,000 previously issued.

Two hours later, in Boston, the trustees of the old trust held the third meeting. Dumaine, now acting as treasurer and trustee of the old trust, reported what had transpired at the two previous meetings. The news was not entirely unexpected, because the trustees had already prepared a plan for the voluntary liquidation of the common stock of the trust. The plan was described to its shareholders in a printed circular bearing the same date. With its consummation, the holding company would own $13,692,700 bonds and 12,316 additional of its common stock, bringing the owned amount to 342,316. This circular, also explained an option by which holders of the common stock of Amoskeag Company, the holding trust, might accept for each share $52 in cash, $40 in the newly issued bonds of the operating trust, and one share of the latter's common stock. When the plan was actually put into effect, common shareholders of the holding company were given until December 6, 1927, to take option of the offer. Exchange of shares was through the Old Colony Trust Company in Boston. About 73 percent of the common shareholders of the old company accepted the offer and exchanged 252,135 shares, leaving 90,181 of that issue outstanding.

While many critics of Amoskeag pointed to this restructuring as a step toward liquidation, an alternative interpretation of intentions of this second financial reorganization was that it was aimed at meeting the needs of both Amoskeag's stockholders and employees through a three-point approach. First, it intended to prevent "corporate raiders" from attempting to purchase Amoskeag stock with the primary intention of making a substantial gain through the liquidation of the holding company's and the manufacturing company's assets. Second, it intended to provide those current Amoskeag Company stockholders who desired to liquidate their holding with a mechanism that would generate more funds than if they sold their stock to outside "corporate raiders." Third, and most important, the intention was to allow the Manchester-based manufacturing company to have an opportunity to survive. The notice was candid:

> This plan places the plant where it should be, upon its own responsibility to succeed or fail. The Manufacturing Company is provided with sufficient means to operate. Bond interest must be earned and paid as well as a reasonable return upon money invested in the business. To accomplish this end the management must institute every possible economy and the community and employees must do whatever is necessary to enable the concern to compete in the market with other mills. Otherwise there can be but one result.

Spinning Room, Cotton

Printing Office

BURLING ROOM, WORSTED

CHAPTER VIII

Amoskeag Manufacturing Company in the Depression

After six years of continued heavy losses, Amoskeag Manufacturing Company reported net profits of more than $500,000 in 1927 and $1 million in 1929. Due to the earnings, the operating company distributed a dividend of $1 on the common and a 5 percent bonus to employees in 1930. That was the only payment in 1927-1931 and as losses in the other three years were more than double the total amount of profit, the final result for the period was a net loss of $1.5 million. Earnings were based not only on manufacturing profit but also on income from investments and land sales.

Market conditions continued to be generally unfavorable throughout most of this period, which ended with the first two years of the nationwide Great Depression. Costs were too high and competition was severe. The company received the cooperation of the city in substantial tax reductions and the employees increased their productivity and accepted several wage cuts. Dumaine reduced his own salary from $100,000 to $40,000, but all the severe efforts came too late to keep Amoskeag's mills profitable. Dumaine repeatedly explained the difficulties of the situation, not only at stockholders' meetings but also in special talks to city officials and employees' representatives.

Cloth production at Amoskeag during the five calendar years 1927-1931 totalled 563.6 million yards, including some 532.4 of cotton and 21.2 of worsted. This amounted to an annual average of 110.7 million yards or about half of the annual average experienced in the five peak years of production of 1912 through 1916. See the breakdown on the next page for the five-year period 1927 to 1931.

CLOTH PRODUCTION 1927-1931
(Years ending December 31)

<u>*Millions of yards*</u>

<u>Year</u>	<u>Cotton</u>	<u>Worsted</u>	<u>Total</u>
1927	136.6	5.6	142.2
1928	96.0	4.0	100.0
1929	109.4	5.4	114.8
1930	105.6	2.7	108.3
<u>1931</u>	<u>84.8</u>	<u>3.5</u>	<u>88.3</u>
Totals	532.4	21.2	553.6

The extent to which management had attempted to diversify the output at the Manchester plant was recognized throughout the industry. Amoskeag was making a wide range of products, from handkerchief and umbrella cloth to mop units. Eighteen types of cotton, rayon and mixture fabrics and four different groups of worsteds were used. For the spring season of 1930, Amoskeag advertised the most complete line of fabrics in its history. Special emphasis was given to rayon dress goods, which included "many fabrics of exceptional merit." Its cotton department offered ginghams, chambrays and a complete line of flannelettes in exquisite colorings, as well as AOA tickings and Hampshires in fancy effects, and towelings. In worsteds there were "staple and fancy effects, in latest weaves and colorings for women's and men's wear." Parkhill fabrics included fine cottons in ginghams and shirtings and also cotton and rayon dress goods.

The company made one of its final efforts to help revive the gingham market in 1927. It contributed $10,038 to an advertising campaign for a special promotion of the formerly favored yarn-dyed fabrics, which had been Amoskeag's mainstay for so many years. In a surprise move in 1928 it announced price reductions on its high quality lines of standard colorfast dress ginghams for fall. There was a vain hope that the lower quotations might make them popular again. Ginghams had been selling below cost for two or three years and some of the best known mills specializing in the fabrics had already been closed, including the Everett and Lancaster, which a few years before had been considered as possible members of a consolidation, together with the Parkhill. An important reason the gingham comeback was not successful was a style trend favoring printed goods rather than yarn-dyed fabrics. As important a factor, perhaps, was that the largest Southern producer of dress ginghams, whose competition had been continually crowding the Northern mills for several years, followed the latter's lead in reducing prices. The result was that the general situation was not much improved, although the Manchester mills were able to dispose of a good amount of its stocks on hand.

The general improvement in the cotton manufacturing industry in 1927 was already evident in the first quarter. Sales were reported to be 35 percent larger than in the corresponding three months of 1926. By April, the mills in New Hampshire were operating at the highest rate of capacity in years. At Amoskeag, the improved outlook was referred to by Agent W. Parker Straw in his conference with employees' representatives early in May. In fact, the manufacturing company reported a profit of $534,561 for the first six months of 1927, compared to a loss of $468,407 in the last half of 1926 and a net gain of $66,054 for the twelve months ending June 30, 1927. A loss of $3.6 million was on the books for the thirteen months for the preceding year.

When reporting the $66,054 profit, Dumaine pointed out that while it represented a tremendous improvement over the preceding period, it had to be kept in mind that there was actually an operating loss of $400,253, and an additional $123,449 was spent on new machinery. The small net profit was made possible because the total of these two items, $523,702, was more than offset by other income of $589,756, which included $439,290 from interest on Liberty Bonds, bank balances and cash discounts, plus $143,208 from sales of land and $7,258 in miscellaneous income. Repairs made at Amoskeag during the year ending June 30, 1927, cost $1,082,225.

Amoskeag's total receipts from sales and other income during the five calendar years (1927-1931, inclusive) amounted to $123.7 million. The $509,776 earned in 1927, after all charges except depreciation, was the company's first profit in seven years. There was another profit in 1929 when the unusually large net of $1,065,535 was reported.

But there were substantial losses in the other three years, especially during the depression of 1930, when the deficit amounted to more than $1.3 million. The company ended the five-year period on the loss side, to the extent of $1.5 million. Amoskeag's continued decline was, of course, accentuated by the Great Depression.

Not only did the company have to dig into previous surplus to the amount of $1.5 million to meet interest requirements, but the surplus was further reduced in 1930 to the extent of $722,198, of which $365,977 was used to pay dividends on the common stock out of profits of the preceding year. No dividends were paid on this issue since 1924 and none were paid after 1930. The other part of the surplus distribution was the $356,221 paid as a bonus to the employees, which was 5 percent of the wages paid in 1929. When these additional payments had been deducted, the total decrease in stockholders' reserves for the period amounted to more than $2.2 million.

COMPARATIVE INCOME ACCOUNT
(YEARS ENDING DECEMBER 31, 1927-1931)
$1,000 $'s

	1927	1928	1929	1930	1931
Sales & Other Income	$28,807	$28,357	$30,283	$19,802	$16,462
Mfg. Costs	27,418	28,456	28,583	20,561	16,718
Mfg. Profit & (Loss)	$ 1,389	($ 99)	$ 1,700	($ 759)	($ 256)
Net Int paid	880	862	635	586	527
Net Profit & (Loss)	$ 509	($ 961)	$ 1,066	($ 1,345)	($ 783)
Bonus & Dividend	0	0	0	722	0
Surplus or (Deficit)	$ 509	($ 961)	$ 1,066	($ 2,067)	($ 783)

THE WAY LEDGERS WERE KEPT IN ANOTHER ERA

In keeping with Amoskeag's practice, the cost of repairs and new machinery was charged to operations. In the years 1927-1931, a total of $5.5 million was spent for such purposes, including $1.2 million for new machinery. In addition, more than $3 million in taxes was paid by Amoskeag in the five years.

Amoskeag by then was not only gradually disposing of its excess real estate holdings but renting unused mills. It leased the 100,000-square-

GENERAL BALANCE SHEET
1,000 $'s

	1927	1928	1929	1930	1931
Assets					
Real Est. & Mach.	$ 16,685	$ 14,595	$ 14,384	$ 14,378	$ 14,374
Cash & Accts. Rec.	5,615	6,690	7,708	9,349	8,105
Inventory	10,173	8,434	8,103	4,429	3,215
Totals	$ 32,473	$ 29,719	$ 30,195	$ 28,156	$ 25,694
Liabilities					
Bonds	$ 14,665	$ 14,665	$ 14,000	$ 14,000	$ 12,463
Payable	44	28	76	49	0
P & L & Reserves	17,764	15,026	16,119	14,107	13,231
Totals	$ 32,473	$ 29,719	$ 30,195	$ 28,156	$ 25,694
Net Current Assets	$ 15,744	$ 15,096	$ 15,735	$ 13,729	$ 11,320

foot wooden weave shed, known as Mill No. 12, to E. R. Apt. Co. In the old Langdon Mill of the northern division, 50,000 square feet was leased to two other concerns.

The City of Manchester's assessment on the company's properties had been $33.4 million in 1926, but by 1931 the tax base was reduced to $18.3 million. The company's portion of the Manchester valuation decreased from 23 percent to 17 percent.

Some records indicate that 85,352 spindles were scrapped, and 12,272 looms dismantled from 1927 to 1931. The disposal of equipment was also illustrated by the fact that in 1921 the company had 1,000 employees in the machine shop and construction department, but by 1929 the number of employees was down to 250, and by 1931, fewer than 100. Statistics for 1929 and 1930 credit Amoskeag with 758,552 spindles, 687,600 cotton and 70,952 worsted, and 22,450 looms, 21,084 cotton and 1,366 worsted, still the largest plant of its kind in the country, but operating only part of the time.

Although there had been evidence of some recovery in the cotton goods industry in the first few months of 1927, management at the end of March of that year reported to the employees' conference that:

> ...every known economy must be instituted, and it will continue to be its aim to see that a high state of individual productivity is maintained, and, when possible, increased.

Agent Straw reiterated that because of the difficult manufacturing conditions management would have to make changes in specific rates where economies could be reasonably made without injustice to the individuals affected. He said that when people were requested to do a greater amount of work, additional compensation would, in some instances where facts warranted, be paid. He suggested that, under the existing conditions, a general wage agreement, such as had been in effect for the previous few years, did not seem advisable at that time, and that no action of any kind would be taken. The matter would be indefinitely postponed. He promised to correct certain situations as a result of grievances. The committee decided to accept the conditions as they existed for another six months. On May 2, when the agent was hopeful about the outlook in the cotton business, 200 employee delegates attended the conference.

But when employees met in October, only a week after the meeting of the holding company, Agent Straw spoke of the general conditions of the industry with particular emphasis on the crisis that the operating concern was passing through. He congratulated the employees for their earnest endeavors to help out the situation by accepting additional work. He cited instances at other New England mills that had liquidated in the past year or so, the Hamilton, Everett, Lyman and Great Falls. He talked about Mr. Carrington's offer of $42 million for the stock of the Amoskeag Company, and reminded them that the liquidation of the mills would have been a devastating impact on Manchester and the State of New Hampshire. For this reason, something had to be done to keep the mills running. The reduction of taxes by the city had helped some, but not enough to pay common stockholders any dividends. After hearing the agent's explanation of the situation, the convention postponed action on the wage question for another six months.

Before adjourning, the chairman moved that a vote of thanks and confidence be given the management for its action in rejecting the Carrington offer. It was carried unanimously. The next convention was a special meeting called by the agent for December 13 to tell them that a reduction in salaries and wages was imperative due to unrelenting competitive conditions and the fact that business in general was so bad. He referred to the capital reorganization adopted in the preceding month and the definite obligations to meet interest charges on the 6 percent bonds, amounting to $880,000 a year. He explained that if the interest was not paid to the bondholders, they could recover the amount of their bonds by having the plant sold. A 10 percent reduction in wages would pay the interest charges on the bonds, he said.

To ameliorate the effect of the wage reduction, management promised to help the cost of living by reducing the rents in the company houses. He said that through an increased work effort the average weekly earnings of weavers, spinners and card room help were approximately the same as prior to the 1924 wage rate reduction. He pointed out that it was clear the mills would not be operating had

Employment office

Telephone exchange

wages not been reduced in 1924. Employees had been fortunate to be working the past two years, even with the reduction. Representatives, however, voted to go on record as being opposed to any reduction in the wage rate and recommended a curtailment of production in line with other New England mills. A committee of five was appointed to meet with Mr. Straw to tell him how the employees felt. On December 15, the agent repeated management's position and said that it did not matter what action the convention took, a wage reduction would go into effect December 24. The convention reaffirmed its action. Considerable discussion centered on whether there was any advantage to continue the representation plan.

The next April, one delegate said that because the employees had not agreed to the reduction, management had no right under the plan to enforce it. Agent Straw said he had no such conception of the plan or the management's obligation to it. The reduction was imperative. He said he felt sure the plan had not been violated in reducing wages by 10 percent. The convention then agreed to postpone indefinitely any suggestion of a wage agreement. From 1924 to 1927, the annual payroll at Amoskeag was practically stationary at $10 million. On October 8, 1924, the company reported 10,000 on the payroll, the majority working on a part-time basis, two or three days a week.

In January 1928, a meeting was held in Dumaine's Boston office. At the meeting were Treasurer Dumaine, Agent Straw and President Lowe. To preserve capital, Lowe suggested the elimination of company pensions. Because the pensions were not pre-funded and the company had no legal obligation to continue the payments, it would only require a board decision to stop all future payments. Straw argued to maintain the pensions. When Dumaine offered to pay the lower grade pensions out of his own pocket as a contribution toward the welfare of the company, the issue was dropped and the pension payments continued until the Amoskeag bankruptcy.

When Dumaine presented his 1927 report at the annual meeting on April 18, 1928, he said that although the manufacturing company showed the largest profit in seven years, its income had not come entirely from the sale of goods. As a matter of fact, the year was generally unprofitable. He didn't expect full operation for the coming twelve months of 1928. Demand was still slack, costs high and competition strong. On the date of the meeting, the mills were operating at 60 percent capacity in the cotton division and 62 percent in the worsted department. Taxes were still too high, he declared, adding that assessments were excessive compared with prices of used machinery on the open market and low plant values noted in textile mill sales. He was grateful for the reduction granted the company in 1927, but a tax of $722,876 was still too much of a burden under existing business conditions. He called attention to the fact that the company had to earn enough to pay interest on bonds as well as a reasonable return on money invested in the plant by shareholders. It was imperative for management to implement every conceivable economy. The community and employees were implored to do whatever was necessary to enable Amoskeag to compete in the market with other mills. Otherwise, liquidation was inevitable. He concluded with the admonition that trustees had no right to continue incurring losses, exhausting assets that belonged to the owners.

On April 21, 1928, speaking at the fourth annual convention of the employees' congress, Dumaine emphasized the necessity of giving shareholders part of the accumulated earnings with the 1927 refinancing. In doing so, he said he was hopeful the company's considerable surplus would cease to become a target of Wall Street interest. He explained that as long as market value of the stock was so much less than the current assets, hostile interests might gain control and force liquidation at a profit only to themselves. He said his plan called for Amoskeag to retain sufficient capital to run the business.

The treasurer declared market uncertainties precluded any wage agreement. He asked one employees' representative, "If he were running the mills, would he not want to know what the market was going to be for the six-month period in order that he might be reasonably sure of disposing of his product at prices which would enable him to pay the wages?" He added that he would not object to a six-month agreement if he could be sure the market would hold and goods could be sold at a profit, but if after making an agreement the market fell off, the mills would have to stop or suffer severe losses in operation.

In July 1928, Dumaine met with Arthur Vining Davis, president of Aluminum Corp. of America to try to convince Davis to construct a new aluminum plant in the greater Manchester area. The Merrimack River's waterpower and the current supply of excess labor made Manchester a desirable location. The following month, Davis notified Dumaine that it was determined the waterpower supplied by the Merrimack was not adequate for the aluminum company's needs. The plant would be built elsewhere. Dumaine and others were solemn.

There was no change in the wage situation at Amoskeag during the next six months. A reopening of the discussion took place in October when the settlement of a four-month strike in New Bedford resulted in changing the previously instituted 10 percent wage reduction to 5 percent. Fall River Mills put their rates in line with New Bedford by a 5.5 percent increase.

Influenced by these developments, Amoskeag employee representatives, at their convention on December 6, 1928, voted to petition the management for a 5.5 percent increase in wages. Agent W. Parker Straw replied that he was in sympathy with the feelings of the employees on the matter, but their request was untimely. He said:

> It is true that there is a healthy demand for our products, but the returns to the company are not so favorable. Business is taken today in small quantities for immediate delivery, and that is the kind of orders that are now on our books. The high cost of quick delivery demanded by the trade is eating into our profit. Furthermore, because of short warps [production runs] and mechanized changes which take more time to get the goods out, more looms have had to be put into operation.

With that pointed out, the convention agreed to table the wage question indefinitely.

Although Amoskeag had 13,843 employees on its payrolls in 1928, because of irregular employment the amount paid in wages was less than in several preceding years. The 8,530 employed in the cotton division and 5,313 in the worsted department received a total of only $8,324,462 in wages in 1928, compared to some $10,000,000 paid in 1924-1927.

That the Amoskeag had no plan for liquidation at that time was emphasized by Dumaine in a 30-minute talk he delivered on the night of February 4, 1929, to a group of Manchester city officials and other leading citizens. But he did explain, in considerable detail, the competition and other problems with which the manufacturing company had to contend. This was Mr. Dumaine's first appearance before a Manchester audience, and the local newspapers reported that he "made a fine impression."

The treasurer explained three factors responsible for the vexatious situation that existed in the textile industry at that time: excessive production, change of styles, and the willingness on the part of some managements to sell below cost. There would be no improvement in the situation until all manufacturers refused to dispose of goods at a loss. Existing prices were below Amoskeag's production costs, he explained. The conditions described existed not only all over this country, but abroad, as well. New England, said Dumaine, had suffered a loss of four or five million spindles and operations in the region were far below normal, only 55 to 60 percent of capacity. The spindles in other parts of the country increased by more than 19 million, operating on an average of 90 percent of capacity.

He called attention to the fact that in the preceding year (1928) the company had to dip into its current assets to the depth of $960,000 to pay taxes, interest on bonds and notes, and to expend $337,000 on new machinery as well as settle current expenses, including payroll. Such action could not be repeated many times, he pointed out, and then referred to the offer made by the company that intended to liquidate Amoskeag at once. Were future operating losses to exhaust current assets, he said, a subsequent takeover offer to liquidate the mills might well find the owners more favorable to a sale. Dumaine promptly added:

> Personally, I am ready to do all that is possible so that we may carry on. I am ready to make further economies to assume all responsibility and stand every criticism to accomplish this. We want to go on doing business. We can't continue at a loss. If you have a remedy for the situation, let me know. Lessening of taxes could be the community's contribution to Amoskeag in this crisis.

The burden of taxation, he explained, made it difficult for Amoskeag to prosper. The plant and machinery were assessed for $12 million but would not bring anywhere near that at a public sale. Present stock quotations represented a value of only $7.5 million for the property.

He said he could not tell the city officials anything about the future prospects. There had been a reduction of production over a period of years. In 1928, only 100 million yards were manufactured. In 1920, when business was at its height, output was 223 million yards. In 1928, gross sales in all departments were only $28 million, compared to $56 million in 1920.

"The only comfort we got out of 1928," said Dumaine, "was that the government hadn't seen fit to put a tax on losses." He concluded with:

> The question for us is to decide whether it is worthwhile tiding this big corporation along until we can operate at a profit again. Sacrifices must be made. Quick capital must not be touched. The owners are willing to help in this critical time, but they won't put any new money into the company. The depletion of quick capital [working capital] means that Amoskeag must go out of business. Don't let us imagine that because Amoskeag has always met its payroll on time and kept its plant intact that it is immortal.

That he preferred to keep the Amoskeag mills in Manchester as long as he could was emphasized by Treasurer Dumaine again at the annual meeting of the manufacturing company on April 13, 1929, when he presented his report for the calendar year 1928. The meeting was one of the largest in several years, with 90 percent of the outstanding stock represented.

"This great textile plant was started here and belongs here," he said. "If I can't make money, I'll do as well as I can." Everything possible would be done to put Amoskeag on a paying basis, he said. If that couldn't be done after a fair trial, then it would be time to discuss liquidation. He reported, as he had reported for the past five or six years, that prospects were not very encouraging. He cited the $700,000 city tax as the greatest handicap in those difficult times.

The following week, April 21, Dumaine attended the fourth annual meeting of the representatives of the employees and management.

He spoke to the mill employees for an hour and a half and gave them the "cold facts" about the Amoskeag situation. In discussing problems of mutual interest in "this typical family gathering," Dumaine emphasized the necessity of economy if the shareholders, employees and the community were to prosper and be successful. He answered all questions put to him by the delegates. It was after 10:00 when he had concluded his remarks, and he was given a flattering ovation. Later in the lobby, with other officials of the company, he met representatives of the 10,000 employees at Amoskeag.

W. Parker Straw resigned as agent on January 18, 1929. A mill career in textiles had been a tradition with this family for nearly 100 years. Following his retirement, Parker Straw was prominent in banking and civic activities. Later he would serve as agent of Amoskeag Industries, the firm that acquired the mills of the Amoskeag Manufacturing Company following the 1936 bankruptcy.

It is generally accepted that Parker Straw's resignation was in response to Dumaine's request. The trustees felt that a new agent might be better able to bring about the economies in production necessary for the long-run survival of the organization.

Following the resignation of W. Parker Straw, Arthur O. Roberts was made general superintendent in charge of operations at the Manchester plant. He had been with the company for about 20 years, including service as head of the worsted division and then as manufacturing superintendent. He later would be elected secretary of the Amoskeag Company following the death of Herman F. Straw.

Henry E. Rauch, an experienced accountant, came into the Amoskeag organization about that time. He had been head of the efficiency or planning department and then the accounting department. In 1930, he succeeded Roberts as secretary of the Amoskeag Company He already held the same office in the operating company. Later, Mr. Rauch became acting agent of the manufacturing organization and continued in that position until the liquidation of the mills in 1936.

During the years 1929-1931, more reliance was placed on individual wage adjustments rather than on general reductions, achieved by several expedients, including increase in job assignment and compulsory overtime at straight-time pay. A plan of "reservation prices" had gone into effect in the summer of 1929. It provided that those employed on a certain type of cloth would be paid at a reduced rate to compete effectively for a given order. A letter to the chairman of the joint committee on adjustment of the cotton section, dated August 13, 1929, explained the situation:

> Competition has forced the company to reduce the selling price on AOA ticking from approximately 22 1/2 cents to 19 cents a yard and employees employed or to be employed on this work, have agreed to accept a reduction of 10 percent in rates and the company agrees for its part as follows: (1) To guarantee full-time work to employees affected for a period of three months, ended December 1, 1929, at which time a renewal of the agreement will be considered. (2) During the life of the agreement to run looms (528) in No. 3 upper weave room on 32-inch ACA, on the basis of 38 looms to the weaver. (3) If, during the life of this agreement, market conditions change, and the manufacturing margin, exclusive of cotton, returns to the basis existing prior to the price reduction, the company agrees to restore the reduction in rates affected by the agreement.

The notice was signed by Roberts and Rauch.

At the employees' congress in October 1929, Rauch appeared before the employee representatives as a personal representative of Dumaine and stated that everything possible was being done to maintain the existing organization. He explained how the company had accepted an order for chambray at a loss in the hope that savings in overhead might be made, but primarily to keep operatives employed full time, if possible. The particular order was for 500,000 yards and the loss was three-tenths of a cent per yard. It was chambrays on which Amoskeag, during the 1922 strike, had lost a major customer in Baltimore, whose business then and later went to the company's chief Southern competitor.

Since Amoskeag's profit in 1929 was partially a result of wage concessions that allowed the firm to accept production contracts otherwise unprofitable at the general wage rate, the company declared a 5 percent bonus in 1930 to all employees "in good standing" during all of 1929. On March 13, the company announced that it would pay the bonus in the form of bank deposits during the first week of May.

Notices were placed in all departments of the mills stating the banks that would accept the deposits. The significance of having the money placed in savings accounts rather then distributing the bonuses in cash was indicative of Dumaine's paternalistic instincts. He was attempting to foster savings on the part of the employees. On the other hand, the employees could simply withdraw the funds and have the same effect as a cash payment.

The bonuses were distributed the first three days of May, and by the end of the third day of distribution more than 75 percent of the bonuses had been withdrawn.

Some six weeks later, the Merrimack River Savings Bank, one of the banks which was authorized to receive the employees' bonuses, was closed by the State Bank Commissioner due to problem loans in the western part of the country. The following week Dumaine reported that Amoskeag Company would reimburse the bonus deposits of those employees in need of the funds. They anticipated that by the end of the following week the paymaster's office would be in a position to verify which funds were still in the bank when it was closed and would be in a position to allow the affected employees to either leave the money in the closed bank until it reopened, have an equivalent sum deposited in one of the other banks, or receive the sum in cash.

Developments in the wage situation at Amoskeag continued on the same basis in 1930. Wage reductions were put into effect in various mills to make it possible to obtain more orders on certain goods. It was made clear that if the reduction was refused, the particular mill would be closed. In August the bag mill would not accept a 10 percent wage cut. It was closed. The point was made. Shortly afterward, the drawing-in department in No. 11 Mill took a reduction that averaged 12.5 percent, to remain in effect for only three months or until the specified order had been completed, but it was prolonged by the acceptance of a repeat order at the same reduced wage rate.

On November 29, 1930, a program was introduced in which each week between 8,000 and 9,000 of the employees still employed at Amoskeag could elect to have ten cents deducted from their pay envelopes to aid those laid off. The company agreed to match the employee contributions and the proceeds were distributed.

Early in 1931, the cotton section was informed that the employees of the bag mill agreed to work the whole year on the existing schedule. From then on, a scheme of reservation rates was developed with special reference to the earlier stages of the manufacturing processes. Only part of the output of the spinning room would be used in producing a "reserved" order. The wage reduction would apply only to that part of the earnings obtained from the production entering into the order.

A six-month general wage reduction of 10 percent was put into effect in the fall of 1931. The company reduced rents the same percentage. In addition, it promised:

> If during any year while wage adjustments are in operation, the company shows a net profit, on a third of such profit it will be divided among employees in direct proportion to their earnings for that year.

Such dividends, it was explained, would be impossible in 1931 due to the losses sustained in the first eight months. Although the employees' convention voted against the wage reduction 2 to 1, the agent, in an address to the convention, offered that he did not believe the 6,000 employees would want to see Amoskeag go out of business. Upon recommendation to the employees' representatives, a vote of almost two-thirds agreed to accept the reduction. The agent gave his thanks, then he gave his word that he would do all he could in return to keep the mills in operation. He would make repairs in various departments, which would make working conditions better, including putting new clothing on cards and Morell rolls in the worsted department, purchase new Crompton & Knowles looms at a cost of $30,000, and a new humidifying system and new rails in the rayon department. These improvements would be classed as new work and gave the mechanical department the benefit of more employment.

An additional 10 percent cut was agreed to by employees in the print cloth department when it appeared the department would have to be closed. There was continued curtailment in the last three months of 1931, particularly in the cotton section. The agent called attention to the huge wage readjustments being made throughout the country, particularly in the South where most of the competition was centered.

He said that management was doing everything possible to reduce costs and that he could see nothing that would help conditions. He suggested that labor on all cotton materials be put on the same basis as print cloths, that is, an additional 10 percent. Before the end of the existing agreement, April 1, 1932, he would ordinarily discuss the business situation with them, but that there was no need to wait until then because they already knew the conditions that were facing them and the company. He added that if it was going to be necessary to liquidate, he did not wish to contract business which would take several months to fill.

When Dumaine, on April 15, 1931, presented his report for the year 1930 to shareholders of the operating company, he noted that the July 1931 would mark the 100th anniversary of the granting of a charter to the Amoskeag Manufacturing Company. He recalled how manufacturing had been tried at the falls for twenty years, but without success, until five men of vision, Ira Gray, Willard Sayles, Oliver Dean, Leonard Pitcher and Lyman Tiffany formed the company under the name that was still in use and started the business that had produced a plant covering two miles of river front. He said, "all honor to those early pioneers. Their courage, skill and foresight deserve our respectful admiration."

In the early days, a smart weaver earned 36 cents a day, Mr. Dumaine said. The payroll in the first year was $36,000, and five years later taxes amounted to the modest sum of $1,770, but in 1920 the company had a payroll of $14 million and in 1925 taxes were $993,000. During the 100 years the total paid out in wages exceeded $300 million and $15 million in city taxes. Dumaine went on to say:

> During the past ten years we have been sailing on a troubled sea which has grown constantly more threatening, and during the past five years has almost wrecked the textile industry in the United States. If the pioneers had been in charge of Amoskeag in that period, they would have needed all the courage and skill that they brought to the solution of the problems of their own day. In these difficult times, without the continued cooperation of the employees, Amoskeag might have been forced to close its doors. Our troubles are not over. There are more spindles in the United States than are required to supply the needs of the people and

> the law forbids any getting together to eliminate wasteful and destructive competition. Reasonable and orderly limitation of production, without raising prices of goods higher than is needed to pay a fair return to labor and capital producing them, could be arranged, if it were not for our rigid antitrust laws. But so long as Congress refuses to modify them, the necessary limitation of production can be attained only by the ruin of the mills and of the communities of which they form a part. Neither the textile worker nor the textile mill owners are receiving justice from our elected representatives.
>
> When I look back and consider what difficulties the founders of the company 100 years ago must have met and overcome, and the trouble that came upon the mills after the Civil War, I find courage to go on, to try to surmount the present difficulties. I find faith to believe that the day will come, if not in my time, then in that of my successor, when your treasurer will stand before you and tell you of success.

When Dumaine made his report for 1931 at the annual meeting of the shareholders of the Amoskeag Manufacturing Company in April 1932, he said management would have to employ fortitude and patience to meet change with change rather than with defiance of the laws of nature and of supply and demand. Due to severe competition, textiles had suffered probably more than all other trades, but thanks to the cooperation of the employees and the loyal support of the community, Amoskeag had been able to survive to that point. Since 1925, the company had been able to pay one annual dividend, but that was merely a single dollar a share. During the same period, it had provided work and maintained an organization it had taken years to perfect, but it had been obliged to encroach upon its surplus to the extent of nearly $7 million.

From January 1, 1932, billings were 37 percent less than in the previous year. Cotton was 4 cents a pound less. Cloth was bringing 10 cents less. If it was demonstrated that textiles could not be produced in New England at a cost to compete in the open market with goods made elsewhere, there would be but one end, he pointed out. A time comes in the affairs of all organizations when it was necessary to pause, survey, and balance the budget. Management determined that time had come. Sufficient business was being offered at the moment to provide work for 6,000 people, but at prices so low that it could not be undertaken at present wages without loss to the company; at lower wages the business could be taken. The question of wages was, of course, for each individual worker to decide. In view of the textile situation in New England, the mills had to be in a position to run without further loss if they were to run at all. The question was difficult to answer. Hasty judgement at such times would affect the welfare of future generations. Management did not want to cease operations to lose the organization built up at great cost. It would prefer to continue to make cloth. But company reserves could not be continually diminished to sell goods at a loss.

In summarizing the five-year history ending in 1931, the reader should appreciate the following facts:

First, the cooperation between management and the employees in the program of "reservation prices."

Second, the decision made by the board to grant a 5 percent wage bonus in 1930 to the employees of record in 1929.

Third, that throughout most of this five-year period, wage concessions in the North to compete more effectively with those of the South were met with further wage cuts by the South.

Fourth, the need for Amoskeag to reduce expenditures for machinery and repairs in an attempt to preserve capital.

Finally, the candor on the part of Dumaine to state that the company could not be expected to continue to run losses in an effort to provide employment and the ultimate obligation of Amoskeag to provide investors with a return on their investment.

The question yet to be resolved: Did the combination of a lower cost of living and lower expectation on the part of the Southern labor force make it inevitable that the South would ultimately cause Amoskeag to cease operations?

THE AMORY MILL

CHAPTER IX

Amoskeag's Bankruptcy

As the income statements for the years 1932 through 1935 show, the Amoskeag Manufacturing Company continued to operate at a loss. During this period, Dumaine became increasingly concerned with the ability of the manufacturing company to generate sufficient cash flow to fund the interest payments for the 1927 refinancing. For this reason, he began repurchasing the bonds in the open market when the price was significantly discounted. Approximately $1.5 million was retired in 1931 with an additional $700,000 purchased in 1932. These repurchases reduced interest payments by about $140,000 per year. The net effect is shown in the following income statements and balance sheets.

COMPARATIVE INCOME ACCOUNT
(Years ending December 31, 1932-1935)
$1,000s

	1932	1933	1934	1935
Sales & Other Income	$ 10,245	$ 13,972	$ 17,096	$ 13,880
Mfg. Costs	11,035	13,514	17,503	14,138
Mfg. Profit & (Loss)	($ 790)	$ 458	($ 407)	($ 257)
Net Int. Paid	420	427	601	855
Net Profit & (Loss)	($ 1,210)	$ 31	($ 1,008)	($ 1,112)

In December 1932, Dumaine drafted a letter sent out by Amoskeag Manufacturing Company's trustees to the current bondholders of Amoskeag's Twenty Year 6% Gold Bonds, due in 1948. Further payment of interest while the company continued to operate at a loss, said the advisory, would reduce the corporation's capital to the point that the bondholder's principal would be at risk. If the net working capital assets fell below 50 percent of the face value of the bonds still outstanding the bonds would be in default and the company could be forced to liquidate. A forced sale might then result in the assets not bringing adequate funds to pay the bondholders their principal. In the best interest of the bondholders and the company, it was recommended that existing 6 percent bonds be exchanged for 7 percent noncumulative preferred stock. The advantage to the company would be that if adequate income were not earned over the next few years, then the preferred dividend need not be paid. The probable advantage to the bondholder would be that if the company were given sufficient time to withstand the depression, then it would become profitable and in a position to meet future dividend obligations, while reducing the risk to principal in the interim.

GENERAL BALANCE SHEET
$1,000s

	1932	1933	1934	1935
		Assets		
Plant Acct.	$14,360	$14,445	$15,110	$14,807
Cash & Rec.	6,928	4,034	7,804	7,586
Inventories	2,811	8,739	7,316	1,754
Other Assets	0	279	222	482
Totals	$24,099	$27,437	$30,452	$24,629
		Liabilities		
Funded Debt	$11,769	$11,463	$11,379	$11,379
Payables	3	1,700	5,716	427
Profit & Loss & Reserves	12,327	14,274	13,357	12,823
Totals	$24,099	$27,437	$30,452	$24,682
Net Working Capital	$ 9,736	$11,352	$ 9,626	$ 9,395

If the bondholders preferred, they could elect an alternative strategy to exchange current bonds for 35 percent in cash and 50 percent in preferred stock. While this second alternative would require the approval of the stockholders, the trustees were willing to make this recommendation to the stockholders if a sufficient number of bondholders were to opt for this alternative. Amoskeag Company was willing to exchange its bonds for the noncumulative preferred if the majority of the other bondholders were willing to do likewise. In a letter dated January 30, 1933, to Gaspard Ferrier, Dumaine wrote, "Looking backwards (always easy) it was a mistake to issue these securities." Dumaine might have been overly critical of himself at this point, since the offer of a preferred stock instead of the bonds in 1927 would not have been successful in combating the potential takeover activity. Few other security holders expressed any interest in the proposed refinancing, so on February 10 the plan was withdrawn.

In March 1933, Amoskeag lowered wages in one additional attempt to bring this cost in line with Southern mills. The rate was maintained until Friday, May 19, when 8,000 employees protested the wage and went on strike. In response, Amoskeag announced that it would close the mills until August 1 when a 15 percent raise would become effective. Apparently the company planned to use this shutdown to dispose of excess inventories, since continual production at the proposed wage rate could not be justified.

The following Tuesday a riot broke out among 4,000 strikers at the company's main gate. In response, four companies of the national guard were mobilized. A second riot was provoked by the arrival of the guard and the result was 70 injuries and 39 arrests near the state armory. Some 2,000 strikers and supporters began throwing rocks. Tear gas had to be used to disperse the crowd.

U.S. Labor Commissioner William Lawler and Bishop Peterson served as intermediaries trying to settle the dispute. The following Wednesday Bishop Peterson announced that the trustees of Amoskeag acceded to his request to immediately grant the disputed 15 percent increase. On Friday of the same week, employees voted 3,623 in favor and 1,184 against the proposal to return to work.

Throughout this time period Dumaine actively was seeking cooperation from Washington. In June 1933, he appeared as a witness on the proposed Industrial Control Act, where he argued for a national policy supporting one 48-hour shift instead of two 40-hour shifts. This position was often favored by Northern mills where the one shift was prevalent as opposed to the two shifts often found in the South. Traditionally, Northern firms found it difficult to recruit labor for the second shift. Dumaine also argued for a uniform labor rate throughout the country. Dumaine received a note from President Franklin D. Roosevelt thanking him for his support of the legislation.

In June 1934, he met with President Roosevelt at the fiftieth anniversary of the Groton School, Groton, Mass. He presented his position in favor of the one shift. While Dumaine acknowledged that it meant fewer hands, he stressed the ability to pay higher wages and to provide steady employment.

In February 1935, Dumaine went to Washington to speak in front of the Cotton Textile Code Authority, an organization authorized under the National Recovery Act to address the issue of wage rate differences between the North and the South. Dumaine, of course, spoke for wage equalization. He then returned to Washington the following month to take up the same issue.

On April 10, 1935, the New England Industrial Committee cited the $2 to $5 weekly wage difference between Northern and Southern cotton mills as the chief reason for the closing of so many New England plants. The council suggested that the citizens of New England write to President Roosevelt requesting an equalization of wages. The Industrial Committee reported:

> A special committee of the NIRA board is now giving considerable study to the problems of the cotton textile industry. The executive order of March 26 limiting certain operations to 30 hours a week had as its purpose the giving of immediate emergency relief to the industry.
>
> As you no doubt know, the future status of the NIRA is soon to be determined by the Congress.

At the April 1935 annual meeting of Amoskeag Manufacturing Company, Dumaine reaffirmed the continuing difficulty of manufacturing in the North. He cited higher taxes and wages paid in New England,

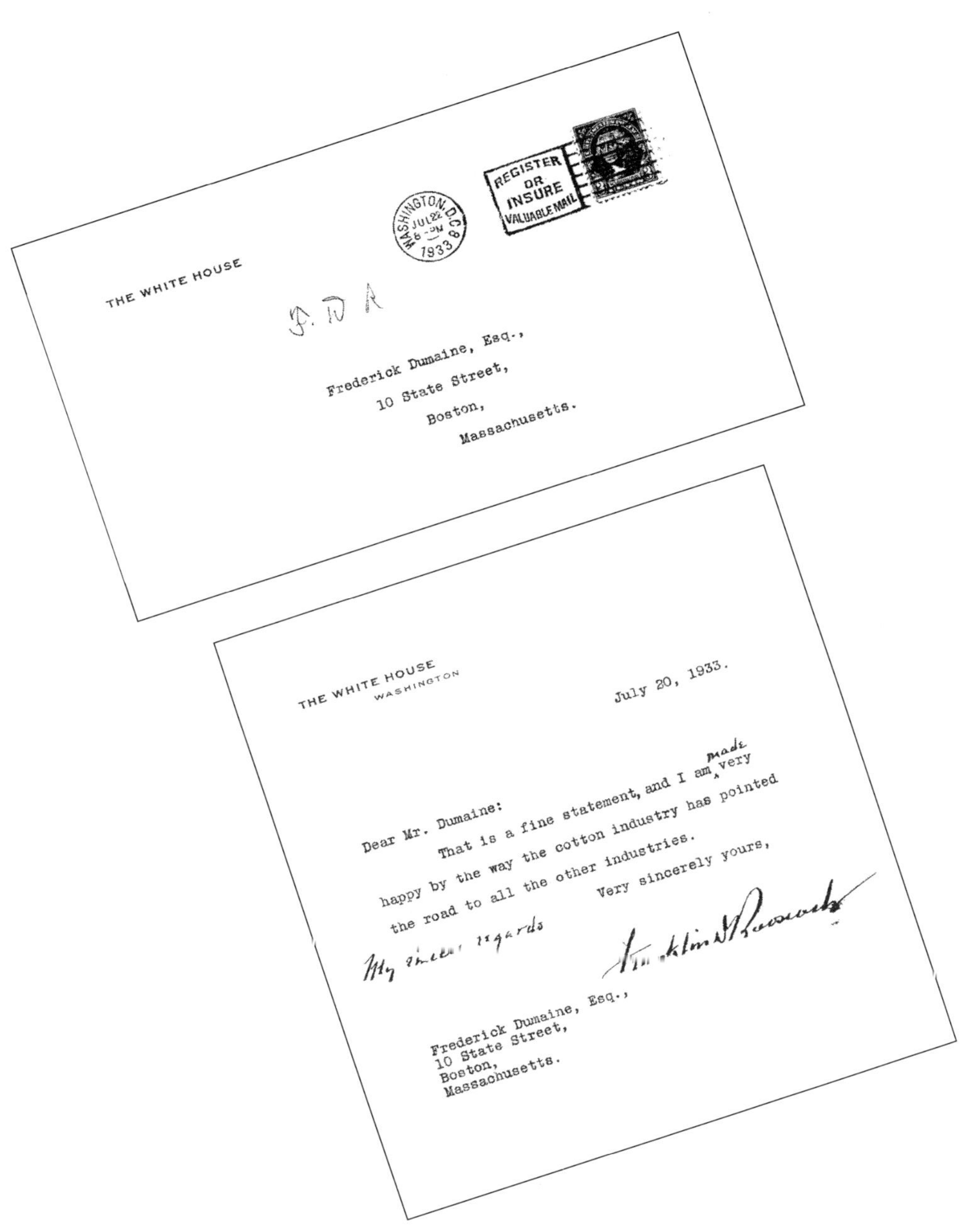

THE WHITE HOUSE

F. D. R

Frederick Dumaine, Esq.,
10 State Street,
Boston,
Massachusetts.

THE WHITE HOUSE
WASHINGTON

July 20, 1933.

Dear Mr. Dumaine:
That is a fine statement, and I am made very
happy by the way the cotton industry has pointed
the road to all the other industries.

Very sincerely yours,

My sincere regards

Franklin D Roosevelt

Frederick Dumaine, Esq.,
10 State Street,
Boston,
Massachusetts.

the periodic labor strikes, and an overall depressed demand for textiles. Of particular significance were the following comments concerning the lower NRA wage scales allowed for Southern mill employees:

> We should pay a living wage, sufficient to provide a comfortable and happy existence. We have no desire to reduce our people to lower standards, but what can our future be if we are unable to bring others up to ours?

For a while it appeared that legislation might produce the equalization of wages that Amoskeag had been seeking since the strike of 1922. However, the South won this political battle and was granted the right to provide employment at a rate below that set in the North. One positive outcome for the North was that the Cotton Textile Code Authority secured permission from the National Industrial Recovery Administration for a 25 percent production curtailment. But, even this victory was short lived when this curtailment, together with all other NIRA policies, was declared unconstitutional by the United States Supreme Court the following May.

In the spring of 1935, Amoskeag began a process of curtailing operations. By September, most production rooms were closed and fewer than 1,000 employees remained in the corporation's employ.

In the same year, Amoskeag began divesting some of its excess property. In March 1935, it razed Langdon Mill No. 1 and two other smaller mills in an attempt to lower property taxes. On June 6, Amoskeag sold Mill No. 12 on North Main St. The fact that this mill, which cost $164,000 to construct in 1902, sold for only $17,500 is testimony to depressed conditions. On July 12, the local newspaper carried an article telling how the corporation sold one of its tenement buildings to the Manchester Building and Loan Association, which intended to raze the building for a new bank on the site. The article noted that it was the first sale of tenement property in the company's history and demonstrated Amoskeag's desire to dispose of some real estate.

Following the September closing, the general public became increasingly concerned with the situation. New Hampshire Governor Styles Bridges appointed a Textile Advisory Board to look into the situation. The committee, headed by Bishop John Peterson, met with local bankers and merchants, labor leaders, union officials and Dumaine. When Dumaine met with the board, he provided a written statement that financial reorganization would be undertaken if:

> (1) Employees would accept the principal of competitive cost basis and operations would be conducted in an orderly and peaceful manner;

> (2) Tasks, rates and speeds could be determined by management to maintain competitive costs; and,

> (3) The company could gain relief from local property taxes.

On November 12, the Governor's Textile Advisory Board submitted its report, which called for greater production efficiency, further relief from local taxes and a new spirit of cooperation between management and employees. The committee opposed wage cuts, one issue considered essential by Dumaine. The rationale for the board's position was:

> To make any general reduction in rates of pay in order to place Amoskeag mill in a better position to compete with low-wage textile centers would be hazardous. Such action would encourage a further lowering of wages in other centers; and the result would be still lower wages in this industry, already underpaid.

However the committee added the following qualification:

> At all events it should be considered only if necessary to make a decision as between a temporary sacrifice and the total closing of the mill.

The Textile Advisory Board stated that the condition at Amoskeag was part of a national problem of overcapacity and argued for national limitations on machine hours and the destruction of less efficient capacity. Moreover, it called for federal action to curb foreign imports.

As for local issues, the board opposed the destruction of mill property to save taxes and suggested that Manchester adopt the "Fall River Plan" in which buildings temporarily not being used for manufacturing were given tax relief. The report also called upon security holders to make sacrifices in order that the mills may reopen.

In September 1935, following the closing of the mills, Dumaine again traveled by rail to Washington. This time he met with Colonel Westbrook to discuss the possibility of the government leasing part of Amoskeag to fill orders that might be allocated to New Hampshire on a noncompetitive bid basis. After hearing of Manchester's plight, Westbrook set up an appointment between Dumaine and Jesse Jones of the Reconstruction Financing Committee. Jones said the government would consider a loan to Amoskeag with the proviso that Amoskeag rid itself of the current bond obligations, which would allow the government to be in a first mortgage position. Because the issue of the bonds was never resolved, Amoskeag never received funding from Washington.

Following the closing of the mills in 1935, Dumaine met frequently with employees and union officials in an attempt to secure a competitive wage rate and orderly operations, one of the essential criterion stated by the trustees for consideration of reopening the mills. In an October 3, 1935, meeting in Manchester, he expressed his hope to avoid liquidation.

> "I will never consent to liquidation until I am confident that further operations of the mills are impossible." He went on to point out that it was Amoskeag that purchased the Manchester Mill and the Stark Mill when they were facing permanent closing, and thereby provided continuing employment to these Manchester employees. However, he cautioned:

> "Is Amoskeag next in line to follow them? I hope not. I lived in Manchester and I have always loved it. I love Amoskeag and I will stay with it until the ship goes down."

On December 16, Dumaine met with Thomas McMahon, president of the United Textile Employees of America, at the Parker House in Boston. At this meeting the two signed an agreement to operate at a competitive cost basis. Two days later, a follow-up meeting was held to establish the basis for calculating the competitive wage.

The executive committee of the manufacturing company met on

December 20 and voted to recommend the trustees file for protection under the bankruptcy act while Amoskeag attempted to reorganize to resume production in Manchester. Four days later the full board met to confirm the recommendation. That same day, the company filed for protection, sending the following notice to its security holders.

The date of the notice — Christmas Eve — so often cited as indicative of Amoskeag's insensitivity in closing the mills, was actually the date that the company **began its attempt to reopen** — *not close* — the mills that actually had been closed since September.

Three days later, Dumaine held yet another meeting with union officials about calculating the competitive wage rate. With no final solution resolved, Dumaine told the union that he must have a decision by January 20, the date of the next scheduled court hearing on bankruptcy. On January 13, one week prior to the deadline, a final meeting was held between Dumaine and McMahon, and the issue was resolved with the union. The matter still had to be voted on by the Amoskeag employees.

At the same time that Amoskeag was negotiating with the union, it was conferring with city officials about property taxes. While Mayor Damase Caron had chastised the corporation for asking for a tax assessment cut in September 1935, by November, following the publication of the Governor's Textile Advisory Board's report, it became increasingly obvious that if Amoskeag were to close permanently the city would generate little tax revenue from the mill property. Amoskeag representatives met with city officials, members of the Citizen's Committee (a local group of concerned businessmen), Bishop Peterson, representing the Governor's Textile Advisory Board, and New Hampshire Chief Justice Robert Peaslee on the tax issue. On December 4, the city announced that it agreed to tax Amoskeag property on a par with competitors' tax rates in the South.

The success in the areas of wage and tax concessions resulted in Amoskeag's trustees feeling confident that it would be able to recommend a formal reorganization plan to its bond and stockholders. At the January 20 bankruptcy hearing, in front of Judge Sweeney, Amoskeag's attorney expressed the opinion that the reopening of the

AMOSKEAG MANUFACTURING COMPANY

BOSTON, MASSACHUSETTS
December 24, 1935.

To the Bondholders and Shareholders of the
AMOSKEAG MANUFACTURING COMPANY.

GENTLEMEN:

The Mills are now closed. Their future must be determined forthwith. Your Company has this day filed a petition under Section 77 (b) of the Bankruptcy Act looking toward a reorganization of the Company.

As set forth in the petition,

"the Company has paid interest on its bonds for many years out of capital. Such payments have totalled about $2,936,000 during such period (5 years). The existence of the outstanding bonds has required the continued payment of interest out of capital, has impaired the credit of the Company, and has resulted, together with other conditions, in making the Company, in the opinion of the Trustees, insolvent. Manufacturing operations can, therefore, no longer be continued on a satisfactory basis. Further payments of interest on the bonds and all payments in full to creditors would constitute a preference inequitable to all other creditors who may not be paid in full; and if continued much longer, payments of interest out of capital would reduce the net quick assets below 50% of the par value of outstanding bonds, thereby constituting a default by the Company under the bond indenture. In the event of any default under the indenture securing the bonds, 25% of the bondholders are entitled to cause the trustee for the bondholders to institute such action at law or in equity as may be necessary or proper for the collection of the sums due and unpaid on the bonds including the appointment of a receiver. Such action would result in enormous loss in values, would in the opinion of the Trustees reduce the recovery to the bondholders, would destroy any future equity that might accrue to shareholders, and would deprive the Company of the means of continuing its operations for the purpose of earning enough to pay off its indebtedness and of safeguarding its shareholders. Reorganization at the present time will leave the Company with sufficient assets and ample credit for possible future profitable operations. The Company, therefore, asks for relief in order to avoid the disaster of such a forced liquidation and in order to obtain reorganization of the capital structure of the Company, which is essential to permit it to continue in business."

There are enclosed herewith a copy of the financial statement and a statement of earnings which are included in the petition.

The history of the business from January 1, 1906 to June 30, 1935, a period of twenty-nine and a half years, was one of profitable operations. The total earnings for these years were in excess of fifty million dollars, and over twenty-three million dollars was distributed during this period in cash dividends to shareholders. In April, 1935, the Treasurer emphasized in his letter to the shareholders the important labor and taxation problems with which the Company has been confronted and which have been important factors in the unsatisfactory results of the last seven years, since the bonds were issued. Every effort has been made and is now being made to work out these problems in co-operation with the employees, the State authorities and the City Government. The Company has been negotiating with all parties and the negotiations have proceeded to such a point that the Company feels these problems will be satisfactorily solved and the necessary co-operation from all sources will be forthcoming.

The Company anticipates that if it is allowed to commence operations again, it will do so only in that portion of the plant which can be economically operated, and that the balance of the plant or machinery not so needed will be disposed of as purchasers can be secured. Such anticipated revision of facilities will not seriously impair the maximum production of which the plant is now capable.

In view of its past record, the Trustees believe that if the Company is reorganized at the present time on a satisfactory basis, its credit will be restored and continued operations will be possible with reasonable prospect of profit.

CHARLES FRANCIS ADAMS
WILLIAM DEXTER
F. C. DUMAINE
F. C. DUMAINE, JR.
WILLIAM C. ENDICOTT
GEORGE P. GARDNER
G. PEABODY GARDNER, JR.
RUSSELL B. LOWE
ROBERT J. PEASLEE
ROBERT G. STONE
FRANK J. SULLOWAY

} *Trustees of the Amoskeag Manufacturing Company*

mill "was not far distant." At this hearing the judge set March 9 as the date for submission of a plan for reorganization.

A meeting was held on February 28 to map out the details of the labor agreement to be voted upon by the employees. In addition to management, union and employees, also attending were Governor Bridges, Bishop Peterson, and former Mayor Arthur Moreau, who represented the Citizen's Committee. The agreement reaffirmed competitive labor rates and no lockouts or strikes. It further stated that violation of the agreement would be justification for discharge; that management would not discriminate because of union membership; and, that local unions would give the international officials the authority to negotiate with management. The union then spent the following week explaining the implications of the agreement to employees on a department-by-department basis. On March 4, in an election overseen by the citizen's committee, the vote was 3,669 for and 3,133 against the labor agreement. Since the strike of 1922, Amoskeag had attempted to establish wage parody with the South. At last, it appeared to be resolved. While all those associated with Amoskeag — the city, the employees and the management — would have preferred to see Southern wages rise to the level in New England, at least a common wage, low as it might be, could provide the mechanism for sustained employment in Manchester.

At the March 9 court date, Amoskeag management submitted its reorganization plan. Key points of the plan can be summarized as follows:

1. General creditors would be paid in full in cash.

2. Bondholders could exchange each $100 bond for either:

    a) One share of first preferred 5 percent stock and 15 shares of common, or

    b) $50 in cash and one half share of second preferred percent stock.

3. Holders of common stock would retain their current holdings.

The notice went on to say that the preferred shares were noncumulative and, as such, would only pay dividends when earned. In addition, if more than half of the bondholders elected alternative B, to take half of their bond in cash, then the corporation would be left without adequate working capital and would have to withdraw the reorganization plan. In effect, the reorganization plan would not proceed if either:

> A majority of the bondholders voted against the plan in its entirety, or

> A majority of the bondholders voted in favor of the plan but elected to turn in their bonds under option B, thus depleting the company of necessary working capital.

That same day, Amoskeag Paper Company owner Frank Carpenter, who had served as a member of the Board of Trustees of the Amoskeag Manufacturing Company from 1906 through 1928, was reappointed to the board. In addition to being one of Manchester's most prominent businessmen, Carpenter was also one of the city's most generous benefactors. Carpenter's acceptance of the post at this time (he was then 90 years old) appears to have been motivated by a desire to serve as an intermediary between Amoskeag and many New Hampshire investors who had mixed feelings about whether they wanted to see the mills reopen under a Boston based management.

The text of Dumaine's letter to the Bondholders Protection Committee was published in the Manchester Union on March 12.

On March 17, the Amoskeag Company announced its willingness to accept the plan and to choose alternative A, provided sufficient other bondholders accepted the proposal to insure the manufacturing company adequate working capital. Since Amoskeag Company owned approximately 32 percent of all of the outstanding bonds of Amoskeag Manufacturing Company, the reorganization plan appeared to be well on its way.

However, the optimism generated by the March 17 announcement received a substantial setback the following day when the combination of a severe rain storm and the seasonal snow melt caused the Merrimack River to overflow the Amoskeag Dam. Substantial flood damage occurred in the mill yard. The city's McGregor Bridge together with four of the Amoskeag's pedestrian and utility bridges were washed out. Severe structural damage to the company's mill buildings was limited to its wooden storage sheds. Despite the fact that all of the mill buildings between the lower canal and the river experienced considerable flooding, they all withstood the storm, a tribute to the quality of the construction over the previous century.

Unfortunately, the machinery inside the mills did not fare as well. The floodwaters carried considerable silt that clogged much of the machinery on the first two floors of the mills in that section of the yard.

The timing of this natural disaster could not have been worse. Considerably more than 50 percent of the bondholders would be required to elect alternative A to leave the corporation with the cash necessary for the assumed working capital, and the additional funds necessary to replace some of the flood damaged equipment.

Dumaine had spent Wednesday, March 18, in New York for a board meeting of the New Haven Railroad. His normal practice was to take the evening train back to Boston. On this occasion, however, he remained overnight in New York. In her unpublished book, Wayman suggests that one reason Dumaine might have remained in New York was the expectation that he might be summoned to Washington to confer with Roosevelt on the possibility of a loan for the Amoskeag. Such a meeting never took place. Son "Buck" Dumaine called him Thursday morning March 19, explaining the severity of the flood. Dumaine took the ten o'clock train to Boston where he was met at South Station by his family to take him directly to Manchester. In his diary Dumaine wrote:

> *Worst ice jam in years. Found 16 feet of water on the dam —
> 5 feet more than in '96 and '97 freshet. All the company's bridges
> gone, as was the Bridge Street bridge. At Granite Street, water
> was over the roadway. For the next 9 hours, the water rose about
> 1/10 of a foot an hour, reaching the peak at 3 a.m. — 17 feet, 2
> inches; where it held for about 5 hours. At 1:15 a.m. our lights
> went off although the power company continued to operate, prob-
> ably from their Portsmouth power.*

When Buck telephoned me at the Biltmore Thursday morning, I instructed him and Chris [Dumaine's second son] to secure all bags in and about Boston and arrange to have them transported by truck without a moment's delay. I forget just how many were used, about 100,000 according to the number of trucks required to land them in Manchester. Detours, roundabout routs, road difficulties, and high water caused the last truckload of bags to arrive after two in the morning and the Manchester supply was nearly exhausted.

Nothing but these bags of sand could have held the flood at both ends of the dam. When the water first started to cover the railroad bed, there was not time enough to remove the tracks and the sleepers. More or less water found its way between the sleepers, causing trouble and anxiety. This is important to remember. Buck and I passed the night with the men, he on the west side, I on the east. Chris was in the sandpit this side of Hooksett. Too much credit cannot be given to Hagan, Ranch, Wheeler, Ahern, Worthern, Peterson, Captain Dunlap of the National Guard, and many others who at great personal risk worked and led the crews. It was a gallant fight and victorious. It has never been realized publicly the extent of the disaster had the 17 feet of water above the 45-foot dam been suddenly freed. In all probability, every city and town in the valley from Manchester to Newburyport would have been destroyed. When the water finally dropped to normal, there were spots on the Jefferson . . and Bag Mill floors where sand and silt were 6 feet deep.

During Thursday afternoon, the authorities closed all bridges and it was necessary to haul sand from Hooksett, four miles. Thirty-odd trucks and 6 to 700 men filled 100,000 bags with sand (the only thing which seems to combat water) and piled them near the gatehouse and across the railroad tracks until the rise ceased. It was nip and tuck which would win. As the crews tired, recruits from militia, C.C.C., and P.W.A. took their places. The same went on at the other end of the dam near the Hydro Station which was saved. Buck was over at that end.

Members of the [Amoskeag Manufacturing Company] staff and many others were on duty 36 to 40 hours without rest. The city government, citizens, and all organizations volunteered and

> *there was the greatest cooperation, unity, and cheerful helpfulness.*
> *They deserve credit for preventing what threatened to be a most*
> *appalling disaster. It was thrilling to see houses and the Hooksett*
> *bridge come down and bound over the dam.*
>
> *The damage is terrible-mostly to machinery, bridges, steam*
> *pipes, and power. Just at the moment the effect upon the future*
> *is hard to determine. My feeling is the bondholders will prefer*
> *cash by all odds and with the expense all this damage has caused,*
> *it seems hopeless to think sufficient funds will be available. Fate*
> *seems to have taken an important part in the situation.*

The pessimism expressed in Dumaine's final paragraph did not last long. One week later, on March 24, Dumaine went to Manchester to plead personally with New Hampshire bondholders to approve the reorganization plan and elect alternative A. At that time he reminded those in attendance that Amoskeag Company had already selected that option. Catholic Bishop Peterson and Episcopal Bishop Dallas urged the cooperation of the local investors. At this time several bondholders stated their need for more time to consider their options.

On April 3, the date of the annual meeting of the Amoskeag Manufacturing Company in Manchester, it was decided to delay stockholder voting on the proposed reorganization plan until a special meeting on April 15, since it appeared that changes in plan would be required as a result of the court hearing to be held on the issue. In the subsequent meeting, the stockholders voted in favor of the reorganization. When Dumaine returned home from the April 3 meeting, he was greeted with a letter from a group of Manchester bondholders stating that unless Amoskeag met certain demands relative to management of the organization, trustee representation and security holder's rites, they would vote against the reorganization and select alternative B if the reorganization was approved by the court.

At the scheduled April 6 court hearing, there were four groups that registered opposition to the plan through their attorneys. Frederick H. Prince, an internationally known financier who held $300,000 of the bonds, opposed the plan, serving notice that he intended to challenge the constitutionality of the bankruptcy laws. Mrs. Eliza Leland, who held $20,000 in bonds, opposed the plan and presented the argument that Amoskeag Company's bondholders in the manufacturing company should be subordinated to all other bondholders. Charles M. Green, a holder of $2,000 of the bonds, objected to the plan stating that it was unfair to bondholders. The United States Trust Co. opposed the plan, holding that if adopted, many of the estates under its trusteeship would suffer losses. Obviously, these groups felt that an immediate liquidation would provide sufficient cash to make this option superior to either alternatives A or B. If the court were to decide, as it eventually did, that Amoskeag Company's bond holdings should be subordinated to all other, then the probability of receiving 100 percent of the bond's face value by all other bondholders was even more likely.

Attorney John Hall, counselor for the manufacturing company, reported that of the $11,377,000 bonds outstanding, about $8 million or 70 percent have accepted the plan, about $1.7 million or 15 percent have rejected the plan and the remaining 15 percent have not been heard from as yet. Of the $8 million accepting the plan, $4.6 million selected alternative A. The remaining $3.4 million selected alternative B. While the results of the vote to accept or reject the reorganization provided the court with over a two thirds majority approval when considering whether to accept the reorganization, the results on the selection of alternative A or B were less than satisfactory. With only 41 percent of the outstanding bonds electing alternative A, the company was short of the 50 percent deemed necessary prior to the flood damage. This was particularly disappointing when it is remembered that 32 percent of the 41 percent of the bonds were owned by Amoskeag Company

Attorney Allen Wilson, representing more than $1.1 million of the $3 million bonds owned by New Hampshire interests, requested an extension in time for his bondholders to consider the proposed plan. These Manchester bondholders were now in an extremely strategic position. If most of the remaining undeclared security holders were to accept the reorganization and elect alternative A, the mills would probably reopen. If a significant number were to reject the plan and/or select alternative B, the mills would be liquidated. At Attorney Wilson's request, Judge Sweeney granted a postponement until April 20.

In an April 11 letter, the Amoskeag Manufacturing Company responded to the Manchester bondholders' demand letter meeting some of the requests and explaining why certain other requests could not be met at this time. The mood of some of the New Hampshire interests may best be represented by the anonymous quote made about this time: "It's time to have Dumaine do what we want him to do."

Dumaine returned to Manchester on April 16 to meet with the local bankers. He pointed out that while the local floods caused $2.5 million in damage, not all of the equipment needed to be replaced at once. Since the company planned to operate at a lower capacity if it reopened the mills, the cost of the repairs and replacement could be spread over the next two or three years. In effect, the trustees of both Amoskeag Manufacturing Company and Amoskeag Company would continue to favor the reorganization plan if sufficient other bondholders selected alternative A. When Dumaine returned home, he found a letter dated April 15 charging that Amoskeag's concessions, as outlined in its April 11 letter, were not sufficient and the Manchester group remained opposed to the reorganization. However, at the April 16 meeting, no one informed Dumaine of this April 15 decision. In any event, the arguments presented by Dumaine and Carpenter resulted in many of these bondholders to reverse their decision and to elect alternative A. By the end of April, both the Boston and Manchester papers indicated that approximately $1 million worth of bonds held by New Hampshire interests were prepared to favor the reorganization.

The following month Amoskeag was faced with two additional setbacks. On May 1, financier Freddy Prince demanded a Master's hearing on the establishment of a priority of bondholders if the company were to be liquidated. In effect, he was supporting the position previously taken by Mrs. Leland that the holding company's bonds should be subordinated to all other bondholders. This would mean that all other bondholders would be paid in full before Amoskeag Company could receive any cash. For any bondholder uncertain whether to select liquidation or reorganization, the potential for such a ruling would tend to create more confidence in selecting liquidation since the likelihood of receiving 100 percent of the bond's face value would be greatly increased. The fact that an internationally known financier supported this alternative gave it increased credibility and attention.

At a May 25 meeting with the mayor and assessor, Dumaine was informed that Amoskeag's property tax obligation for the year would be $280,000. This was $140,000 or 100 percent above the amount that Dumaine said he believed was agreed to at a meeting the previous December, when it was decided to tax the plants at a rate comparable with Southern mills.

When the trustees met on June 1, it was reported that owners of $5,603,540 or 49 percent of the total bonds outstanding elected alternative A. The following table summarizes the breakdown of these bonds.

While 49 percent is quite close to the 50 percent designated as necessary by Amoskeag when it first proposed the reorganization plan, it was prior to: the increased expenditures required by the flood; the partial reversal of the tax concession by the city of Manchester; the

BONDS CHOOSING ALTERNATIVE A

Bond Holder	Total Bonds Held	Alternative A Bonds	Alternative A Percent
Non-Amoskeag Company			
New Hampshire	$ 3,000,000	$ 1,500,000	50
All Others	4,780.000	507,000	11
Total	$ 7,780,000	$ 2,007,000	22
Amoskeag Company	3,597,000	3,597,000	100
Total	$ 11,377,000	$ 5,604,000	49

lack of less than full support by the community's business leaders; the movement to subordinate Amoskeag Company's bonds to all other bonds in case of liquidation; and, the failure to receive financial assistance from Washington.

According to son "Buck," as detailed in the preface, there was a subsequent meeting between Dumaine and Manchester investors two or there days prior to the opening of the final bankruptcy hearing. Whether "Buck" was confusing this date with the April 15 meeting is unclear. Amoskeag records prove that many Manchester bondholders who opposed the refinancing at the April meeting reversed themselves and agreed to go along with the refinancing. Whether there was an additional reversal cannot be determined. However, a significant number of the bondholders still opposed the refinancing.

The intent of the Manchester investors unwilling to accept the refinancing plan at the time is unclear. Their decision could have been based on a strict fiduciary obligation for the funds entrusted to their care. It could be they felt that they stood a better chance of regaining the funds, if Amoskeag were put into receivership, particularly if bonds held by Amoskeag Company, were subordinated to all other bonds. Alternatively, they could have seen this as an opportunity for Manchester to rid itself from the control of Dumaine and Boston interests. They might have anticipated that local citizens would be able to purchase the mills at bankruptcy prices as was effectively done. Regardless of their reasoning Amoskeag was left with an insufficient number of bondholders willing to support the plan to make the proposed refinancing feasible.

On June 9, the day prior to the opening of the final bankruptcy hearing, the minutes of the special meetings of the trustees of the Amoskeag Manufacturing Company and the Amoskeag Company read as follows:

Amoskeag Manufacturing Company
Boston, Massachusetts

June 9, 1936

A meeting of the Trustees of Amoskeag Manufacturing Company was held in Treasurer's office, 10 State Street, today, at 10:30 A.M.

Present:
Messrs. Frank P. Carpenter
William Dexter
F.C. Dumaine
F.C. Dumaine, Jr.
George P. Gardner
G. Peabody Gardner, Jr.
Russell B. Lowe
Robert G. Stone

and by invitation:
Richard C. Curtis
John L. Hall

Minutes of previous meeting were read and approved.

Progress of the Company's Reorganization was reviewed and upon consideration it was

VOTED:
Because the net quick assets of the Company will be depleted by reason of the fact that so many bondholders have elected to withdraw half of their bonds in cash under Alternative B of the Plan of Reorganization, particularly in New Hampshire, and the fact that the recent flood will necessitate the expenditure of about two and one-half million dollars before the Mills can be operated, and because of other material factors, the Trustees can no longer recommend the Plan.

Messrs. Frank P. Carpenter and F. C. Dumaine, Jr. voted against the foregoing motion and F. C. Dumaine did not vote.

There being no further business the meeting adjourned.

F. H. Smith, Clerk

AMOSKEAG COMPANY
Boston, Massachusetts

June 9, 1936

The adjourned Trustees' meeting was held in the Treasurer's office, 10 State Street, today, at 11:00 A.M.

Present:
    Messrs: William Amory
        Frank P. Carpenter
        Charles E. Cotting
        William Dexter
        F. C. Dumaine
        F. C. Dumaine, Jr.
        George P. Gardner
        G. Peabody Gardner, Jr.
        Robert G. Stone

        and by invitation:
        Andrew Marshall

Minutes of June 1st meeting were read an approved.

Present situation of Amoskeag Manufacturing Company Reorganization was reviewed and copy of vote passed by that Company's Trustees, indicating the Reorganization Plan to be no longer feasible, due to the large number of Bondholders electing Alternative B of the Plan and conditions caused by the recent flood, submitted.

Upon consideration it was

VOTED:

    That it having been determined by the Trustees of Amoskeag Manufacturing Company that the Plan of Reorganization filed by that Co. as Debtor in the proceedings under Section 77B in the United States District Court at Boston may in their judgment no longer be considered as feasible, on account of the damage done to the property of that Company by flood since the filing of said Plan, and greatly accelerated expenditure from its quick assets for repairs and reconstruction if the plant were to be operated, and on account of the further shrinkage of quick assets which would result from the election of Option B rather than Option A which has been made by a disappointingly large number of bondholders, and the failure of more than one half in amount of the New Hampshire bondholders to leave their money in the business by election of Option A, and the uncertainty in other factors materially affecting the business and finances of that company, now therefore in view of the foregoing facts and with due regard for their obligations as Trustees of this Company that they cannot now in the exercise of their best judgment favor the approval of said Plan of Reorganization.

and further

VOTED:

That the firm of Hutchins and Wheeler be authorized and instructed as attorneys for this Company to inform the United States District Court of the foregoing vote, and to take such steps as may be necessary and proper for withdrawing the assent previously given by this Company to the Plan of Reorganization filed by Amoskeag Manufacturing Company, Debtor.

F. C. Dumaine, Jr. desired to be recorded as against the two foregoing motions and Messrs. Frank P. Carpenter and F. C. Dumaine did not vote.

There being no further business the meeting adjourned.

E. H. Smith, Clerk

COVER OF THE 1912 BOOK BY THE MANCHESTER CHAMBER OF COMMERCE.

Chapter X

Critics of Dumaine's Stewardship

Following Amoskeag's bankruptcy, critics of Dumaine attributed the demise of the corporation to:

1) the expansion of output through the acquisition of existing mills rather than through internal growth;

2) the financial recapitalization of 1925 and 1927;

3) the subsequent issue of watered securities; and,

4) overall poor management practices during the twentieth century.

While most of these critics acknowledge the problems associated with the cost advantages of Southern manufacturers, they suggest that alternative decisions on the part of Dumaine would have enabled the corporation to operate profitably in the long run and thus save manufacturing in the City of Manchester. This writer contends that the cost advantage of Southern competition was the **only** reason for the eventual closing of the mills. All of the decisions on the part of the corporation, which have been so severely criticized in the past, have stood the test of time and have proved to be the best actions and decisions that could occurred.

The causes of failure will be examined here in their historical context to illustrate the impact of increasing competition from Southern manufacturers that would force the closing of Amoskeag.

I. THE METHOD OF EXPANSION

Creamer and Coulter, in their WPA National Research Project[1] assert that one primary reason for the failure of Amoskeag to operate profitably in the long run was a result of its method of expansion in the twentieth century. They conclude that Amoskeag would have been more competitive if growth had been by way of construction of new plants, rather than by the acquisition of existing mills in which there was inherent obsolescence in equipment.

As delved into earlier in this book, three principal external expansions were undertaken in the twentieth century. The first was in 1906 when Amoskeag acquired the Manchester and the Amory Mills. The second occurred in 1922 when Amoskeag purchased the Stark Mill. The final external expansion was in 1925 when Amoskeag merged with the Parkhill Mills. We will examine each.

The Acquisition of the Manchester and Amory Mills

In 1906, Amoskeag acquired both the Manchester Mills and the Amory Manufacturing Company. To place the size of this acquisition in context, it is important to understand that prior to the merger Amoskeag had 8,000 employees while Manchester Mills had up to 3,000 employees and Amory Manufacturing Co. had 1,400. Amoskeag, however, maintained an extensive machine shop for the manufacture of textile equipment. Because of this, the ratio of textile operators among Amoskeag and the merged firms would be somewhat less.

At the time of the merger, the stock of the two acquired firms was purchased for cash. However, the stockholders who turned in their shares for cash were allowed, at their discretion, to purchase new shares of Amoskeag equal to a major portion of their cash proceeds from the sale of their stock to Amoskeag. A total of 17,600 shares of Amoskeag stock were issued for $3,520,000. Amoskeag, then, only paid $1,555,000 in cash for the acquisitions.

As to whether the manufacturing facilities were equipped with state-of-the-art machinery, it is important to study the long-term relationship of these two corporations with Amoskeag.

The Amory Corp. was incorporated in 1879. At that time, it purchased the land for a nominal price from Amoskeag and contracted for construction of both plant and equipment by the Amoskeag Manufacturing Company at what was described as unusually attractive price. The board of Amory Corp. had many shared directors with Amoskeag. Notices were sent to the existing stockholders of Amoskeag informing them of the contractual arrangement and allowing them to purchase stock on a prorated basis to their current holding in Amoskeag.

The net effect was that Amoskeag shareholders could invest in a second smaller manufacturing facility without subjecting their original investment in Amoskeag to additional risk. While this method did allow for the possibility that the stockholders could sell their shares in one or the other corporations and thus create a divergence in interests, over the entire life of the Amory Manufacturing Co. there continued a strong duplication on the boards and the two companies shared a common management.

The original Manchester Mills preceded the construction of the Amory Mills. In 1839, the corporation was organized as the Merrimack Mills and later renamed Manchester Mills. As with the Amory, it shared common stockholders and directors with Amoskeag. It also had its building and some of its equipment produced by Amoskeag. This endeavor did not meet with the same success as Amoskeag and Amory, however, and in 1874 the property was bought by the newly incorporated Manchester Mills. This occurrence highlights the shrewdness in the concept to form separate corporations when Amoskeag interests diversified its production into print cloth. The basic operation of the Amoskeag Mills was not affected by this sale.

From 1874 until 1903, the Manchester Mills were managed by a different group with no shared directors. This corporation, with a capitalized investment of $2 million, met with mixed success. While it did succeed in paying dividends over most of those years, by 1903 it was in need of substantial additional capital. The directors of the Manchester Mills approved the issue of $2 million new preferred stock to which existing common stockholders could subscribe on a prorated basis. Very little interest was shown on the part of its current shareholders. Jefferson Coolidge, then president and prior treasurer of Amoskeag, offered to subscribe to all the new securities under the condition that the current shareholders reduce their original $2 million capital to $500,000. In effect, every four shares of $100 par value would be replaced with one share of $100 par. At the same time, Coolidge offered to acquire all outstanding shares of common stock at $25 per original share or $100 per new share. This offer was accepted by the Manchester Mills shareholders. The net result was that Amoskeag interests acquired the entire Print Works facilities for $500,000 and subsequently invested an additional $2 million for future capital improvements.

On the same day the stockholders accepted Coolidge's offer to purchase the new stock issue, the board of directors was replaced by an Amoskeag board. Frederic Dumaine, then an employee in the Amoskeag Treasurer's office, was elected treasurer of the newly organized Manchester Mills. During the next 30 months over $1 million was spent on new equipment. In his October 1905 report to the directors of Manchester Mills, Dumaine stated:

> The managers directly in charge of the operations at the mills feel confident the concern is now thoroughly first class and up-to-date in every important detail. Many economies have been inaugurated, departments concentrated, and all possible savings in running expenses made.[2]

An examination of the records of the directors' meeting of the three corporations involved in the 1906 merger leads the writer to conclude that these acquisitions were not arbitrary expansions through the purchase of questionable mills and equipment. Rather, they represented the reacquiring of production facilities that physically abutted the property of Amoskeag. Further, the mills acquired represented state-of-the-art machinery or they were immediately refurbished to that state through external purchases and internal production of new textile equipment.

The Construction of the Coolidge Mill

The Coolidge Mill was constructed in 1909. This expansion was similar to most growth in the nineteenth century in that it was through new construction rather than through acquisition. This is the type of growth that Creamer and Coulter said they feel should have been utilized in the twentieth century. Since there is no criticism of this growth, there is no need to defend it. The fact is mentioned here simply to present a complete picture of growth in this century. The new mill was equipped with the latest in machinery and resulted in increasing overall mill capacity from 160 to 240 million square yards of cloth a year. The construction further illustrates Amoskeag's long-term plan to continue production in Manchester rather than building new facilities in the South.

The Acquisition of the Stark Mill

The Stark Mill, like Amory and Manchester, was constructed on land purchased from Amoskeag. The Amoskeag Manufacturing Company constructed the buildings and manufactured much of the original textile equipment for Stark. The directors and management were common to those in Amoskeag through the nineteen century. In 1901, Amoskeag interests sold the Stark Mills, which became a subsidiary of U.S. Cotton Duck. By 1922, U.S. Cotton Duck had been reorganized as the International Cotton Mills, which controlled plants in Georgia, New York, Massachusetts and Canada.[3]

In 1922, both Amoskeag and Stark employees, like many other employees throughout New England, were on strike protesting the wage cuts and workweek expansions imposed by Northern manufacturers. New England mill owners collectively made these labor policy changes to enhance their ability to compete with the labor conditions that prevailed in the South.

During the strike, Amoskeag had the opportunity to acquire the physical assets of the Stark Mills. Since Stark represented the only other significant textile employer in Manchester, this acquisition gave Amoskeag a monopoly position relative to mill labor in the city. More important, it seems illogical to cite the acquisition of the Manchester plant of a nationwide firm which was in the process of shifting production to the South, as a contributing factor to decreasing Amoskeag's ability to maintain employment in Manchester.

The Parkhill Acquisition

By 1925, Amoskeag had experienced three years of unprofitable operations. At this time, the company decided to reorganize into two separate trusts. The new trust, named the Amoskeag Manufacturing Company, retained all of the physical assets associated with the manufacturing and some $6 million in cash and government securities, which represented about a fourth of the cash surplus held by the old trust. The old trust — renamed Amoskeag Company from its former name Amoskeag Manufacturing Company — retained $18 million in government securities. In return for the cash surplus and physical assets put into the new trust, Amoskeag received 92 percent of the stock in this new trust. The remainder of the ownership went to the principals of the former Parkhill Manufacturing Co., whose mills in Fitchburg, Mass., were merged with the Manchester Mills into the new Amoskeag Manufacturing Company. This expansion is different from all the previous expansions because it represented additional capacity outside of Manchester. In fact, all the previous additions represented property that physically abutted existing Amoskeag property.

The exact intention of this merger seems unclear on the part of Amoskeag's critics. An examination of the bankruptcy proceeding leads this writer to the conclusion that this was the beginning of an attempt to establish a monopoly position in the New England production of gingham. In response to a question as to why the plan for reorganization in 1935 called for some $600,000 in cash when Amoskeag had originally set aside $6 million at the time of the 1925 reorganization, Dumaine said the following:

> I told you in the beginning that we were trying to buy up a lot of other properties. We made the trade with the Parkhill, and when we capitalized that thing we had it in mind that one or two other organizations might be available, and we set that money aside for the purpose of having the money to carry out the trade. When we got through with our examination of these other two properties which we were looking at and sat down with the gentlemen who owned them, the prices they asked for their properties, as we viewed them, were much in excess of anything that we would want to pay. And as that whole picture had been wiped out it was not necessary for the mill, the Amoskeag Manufacturing Company, to have $25 million of working capital. And we had always figured with the normal business that it did, that it required between $15 and $16 million. That is the reason of the change.[4]

Critics of the Parkhill acquisition note that the Fitchburg mill property was sold merely three and a half years later for a fraction of the purchase price. While this final acquisition did not prove to be Amoskeag's most successful, it is important to note that Amoskeag did not invest one dollar of cash in the purchase. Rather, the Parkhill property was merged with the new Amoskeag Manufacturing Company through an exchange of stock. Whether this acquisition had a positive or negative effect on the ownership of the original stockholders of the old trust, it had little impact on Amoskeag's long-run financial strength.

Evaluation of the Twentieth Century Method of Expansion

The following table on the number of active spindles in the United States sheds considerable light on the advisability of Amoskeag's method of expansion in this century. One should seriously reassess the preference toward internal growth on the part of New England textile firms. It appears that expansion through the purchase of existing capacity at an appropriate price might be the best method. This would be particularly true when the acquired facilities would be put to a critical appraisal of existing equipment combined with refurbishment or replacement when warranted. There appears to be little justification for assuming that Amoskeag's strategy in this area was

TABLE I[5]

NUMBER OF ACTIVE SPINDLES

(thousands)

Year	New England	South	South as a Percent of New England
1870	5,498	327	5.9
1880	8,632	561	6.5
1890	10,935	1,570	14.4
1900	13,171	4,368	33.2
1910	15,735	10,494	66.7
1920	18,287	15,531	84.9
1930	11,351	18,586	163.7
1935	7,763	18,096	233.1

anything but optimum, given the company's knowledge of the facilities involved and its own capacity to refurbish existing equipment or purchase new machinery when necessary.

II. THE FINANCIAL RESTRUCTURING OF 1925 AND 1927

Creamer and Coulter[6] and Sweezy[7] cite the financial restructuring of 1925 and 1927 as instrumental in the Amoskeag's eventual bankruptcy. They hold that the withdrawing of reserves in 1925 and 1927 left the corporation with inadequate working capital with which to face the lean years ahead. Further, they contend that the 1927 substitution of preferred stock, whose dividends could be passed in periods where it was necessary to preserve cash, for bonds, whose interest payments must be met, further handicapped the company. To examine these issues, it is necessary to review the history behind the actual refinancing and then address the criticism cited.

History of the Amoskeag Refinancing

Throughout its history, Amoskeag followed a practice of expending nearly all capital projects. From 1906, when the Amory Mills and the Manchester Mills were acquired, until 1925, the year of the first recapitalization, the fixed assets were recorded at a nominal value of $3 million despite the investments on the Coolidge Mill, the bag mill, the power plant and the Stark Mills. By 1925, replacement costs, before depreciation, were estimated to be almost $50 million.

In addition, Amoskeag followed a practice of conservatively estimating inventories and receivables. By 1925 that practice resulted in working capital being understated by an additional $10 million.

Due to limited financial data published by the company, combined with the accounting practices of expending all capital projects and of understating inventories, it is impossible to adjust its reported income during these years to reflect what earning would have been using conventional accounting practices of today. It is appropriate to say that over the entire period the earnings would have been substantially higher.

In the years preceding World War I, management at Amoskeag was aware of the increasing production by Southern manufacturers that had the advantage of lower labor costs and proximity to raw materials. During the war, Amoskeag, like other manufacturers in both the North and South, experienced unprecedented prosperity. At the end of the war, Amoskeag had accumulated U.S. Government Bonds with a market value of $28.9 million.[8]

Following the war, profits dropped substantially. The fiscal year ending May 31, 1924, showed a loss of $2.9 million. That same year, Dumaine stated in his October 24 letter to shareholders:

> The trustees at a meeting held today concluded that prudence and the best interest of the concern compelled them to omit the dividend upon common shares, usually paid at this time. The losses of the past year and the uncertainty of the cotton industry, for the immediate future, make the passing of the dividend imperative.[9]

On August 25, 1925, the directors called a special meeting of the shareholders to vote on a proposal to separate the current Amoskeag Manufacturing Company into two separate trusts. The original trust would be renamed the Amoskeag Company and the new trust would be called the Amoskeag Manufacturing Company. At the same time, the Parkhill Mills in Fitchburg, Mass., would be merged with the Manchester, N.H., mills of Amoskeag in the new trust. Amoskeag Company ended up owning 92 percent of the new trust with Parkhill interests owning the remainder.

For the purpose of determining the relative contributions of Amoskeag and Parkhill interests, the properties were appraised on a replacement cost minus depreciation basis. The Manchester property was assessed at $33 million while the Fitchburg property was valued at $3 million. Based on this appraisal, Amoskeag Company, the old trust, received 330,000 shares of no par common stock in the new trust. The Parkhill principals then received the remaining 30,000 share of the no par common stock issued at that time.

It is important to understand that the $36 million value for fixed assets, which appears to be a legitimate appraisal based on the method used, was never practiced in subsequent reporting to shareholders by either the new or the old trust. Instead, the fixed assets were carried at the net book value that had been established when the federal income taxes were imposed and the company needed a basis for calculating depreciation. Based on this new stated value, the company continued its practice of not reflecting the impacts of depreciation or new capital investments on its income statements. In effect, depreciation expenses were not included in the cost of goods sold. On the other hand, any subsequent capital investments were treated as expenses in the year in which they occurred. While this approach may not have been the optimum, the shortcomings tended to offset each other and the financial statements explained the methods used.

At the time of this recapitalization and merger, a physical appraisal of the current assets was also conducted. The value of those assets put into the new trust by the old Amoskeag trust was determined to be approximately $26.5 million and the old trust received 264,720 shares of no par preferred stock in the new trust. Amoskeag's contribution represented an increase of about $10 million in receivables and inventories over the value that had been carried on Amoskeag's book. Parkhill's contribution in this area was determined to be about $2 million for which it received 202,800 shares of the no par preferred stock in the new trust.

In effect, the old trust turned over all of its mills, inventories and receivables, together with some $6 million in cash and government securities, in exchange for more than 90 percent of the stock of the new trust. In the process, the old trust withdrew the remaining $18 million in government bonds and other investments from the manufacturing company.

A comparison of the cash and security balances following the formation of the new trust with the balances that existed prior to the high profits generated in the war years indicates that the $5.5 million in government bonds left in the new trust represented excess working capital, which was either set aside to offset expected future poor performances or to provide the trust with a ready cash balance with which to purchase additional textile manufacturers, as suggested by Dumaine in his testimony in the bankruptcy hearings. No similar comparison can be made as to whether the balances in other working capital were excessive relative to prewar levels, since the amount of understatement of these accounts in the prewar years cannot be determined.

Because the old trust owned more than 90 percent of the stock of the new trust, with the remaining percentage held by a few Parkhill interests, the stock of the new trust was not listed on a stock exchange. However, the old trust continued to be traded on the Boston Stock Exchange.

On October 28, 1925, two months following the formation of the new trust, Amoskeag Company, the old trust, issued its report to shareholders. The report is significant in two respects. First, in reporting the balance sheet of the old trust, the holdings of stock in Amoskeag Manufacturing Company were not included among the firm's assets. Instead they were footnoted below the balance sheet with the following explanatory statement:

> No value has been placed upon the shares of the Amoskeag Manufacturing Company held. It must of necessity be entirely problematical, and continue so until the company's earning power can be demonstrated.[10]

The second significant factor in this annual report was the pessimistic outlook for future earnings in the manufacturing subsidiary. After citing a $1.55 million loss, the report went on to say:

> We are all more interested in future prospects than in anything else, and I regret that I cannot give you much encouragement. At the present moment, as for many months past, light consumption, constant changes in styles, high costs and ruinous competition between producers make profitable operation impossible. Periodical depressions in this industry have often occurred in the past. Except for its severity and long continuance, the present depression is not very different from others we have experienced. If the Amoskeag had not laid aside in good times a reserve with which to meet bad times, its position would indeed be perilous. As it is strong financially and in good condition physically, there is reason to believe that it will be able to take advantage of any change in the market.[11]

After discussing the need for property tax relief in order to better compete with Southern manufacturing and commenting on the past accomplishes of the company, Dumaine noted:

These results have not been attained by distributing all the earnings but by applying a reasonable part, in good years, to the improvement of your property and the accumulation of a reserve for bad years, such as we are now going through. The great majority of the shareholders have concurred in this course, which is the only one consistent with their real interests. I do not know of any mill which has so conclusively demonstrated the soundness of this method. Plenty of instances will occur to you of mills which have amply proved the unwisdom of any other course. I hope that the next twenty years will show as good results as the past, by the consistent application of the principles and practices which have succeeded in improving your property, paying suitable dividends and putting your company in a position to ride out the worst storm the textile industry has ever known in this country.[12]

It is important to recall that the state of the textile industry, described by Dumaine, existed prior to the beginning of the Great Depression.

The performance of the manufacturing company following the 1925 restructuring was improved but was less than satisfactory. While the subsidiary earned a profit of $66,000 for the fiscal year ending June 1, 1927, this was after interest earned on the firm's government bonds. If one subtracted the interest earned, the new trust continued to lose money on its manufacturing.

In the fall of 1927, the Amoskeag Company received an offer from Curtis, Sanger and Company to purchase all the outstanding shares of the old trust with the intent of closing the mills and selling the assets for a quick profit. While the trustees declined the offer, they were cognizant of increasing stockholders' dissatisfaction with the current earnings and future outlook of the manufacturing portion of the combined trusts. As the majority stockholder of the manufacturing company, the parent company exercised its power and elected to retire the 285,000 preferred stock for $8,135,076 in cash, $14,665,000 in 20-year, 6 percent bonds and 13,191 additional common shares in the new trust. As a result of this exchange, the old trust, which had previously owned 93 percent of the preferred stock of the new trust, received a cash inflow of almost $7,600,000. In addition, it came into possession of $13,692,700 worth of the 6 percent bond issued and

12,316 more shares of common stock, increasing its total common stock ownership to 342,316 shares.

Trustees of the old trust, which had 93,843 preferred shares and 242,316 common shares of its own stock outstanding made the following offer to its stockholders on November 21, 1927:

> To such of the Common Stockholders as wish to avail of it, they offer, at any time until December 6, 1927, For each Common Share of Amoskeag Company
>
> $52 in Cash
>
> $40 in 6% Amoskeag Manufacturing Company Bonds
>
> 1 Amoskeag Manufacturing Company Common Share.[13]

The trustees pointed out that this recapitalization had two objects in mind.

> 1. To distribute to such Common Shareholders as wished their proportion of the Company's assets, thereby preventing anyone else acquiring them below their true value;
>
> 2. To secure the continued operation of the works to Manchester and New Hampshire without danger of wasteful wrecking.
>
> The plan places the plant where it should be, upon its own responsibility to succeed or fail. The Manufacturing Company is provided with sufficient means to operate. Bond interest must be earned and paid as well as a reasonable return upon the money invested in the business. To accomplish this end the management must institute every possible economy and the community and employees must do whatever is necessary to enable the concern to compete in the market with other mills. Otherwise there can be but one result. The plan now presented is the result of long and careful consideration and has been adopted by the Board as being, in their judgment, advantageous for the Shareholders.[14]

Some 252,145 shareholders in the old trust exercised this option, leaving Amoskeag Company with 90,171 shares or 23 percent of the stock in the new trust. In addition, it held $3,606,900 or about 25 percent of Amoskeag Manufacturing Company's new bond issue.

In the process, Amoskeag Company paid out to these shareholders some $13.1 million in cash or $5 million more than it had received from the retirement of the manufacturing company's preferred stock.

Evaluation of the Amoskeag Refinancing

Creamer and Coulter stated that in the reorganization of 1925 the trustees were clearly embarking on a course of liquidation. Further, that the refinancing of 1927 was a scheme to help stockholders hedge their position by salvaging what they could in cash and bonds while maintaining common stock in the event that the manufacturing company were to be successful. Creamer and Coulter question the legitimacy of stating that the retirement of the preferred stock partially represented a true savings in future capital outflows because the preferred dividends need not be paid if the company did not generate adequate earnings, while the interest on the bonds still had to be paid. In effect, they contend that the subsequent interest payments represented partial liquidation.

Sweezy offered that those directors aware of the problems facing the New England textile firms had two choices: to liquidate or to invest the resources accumulated in the past to cover losses and to allow further equipment modernization. He describes the refinancing of 1925 and 1927 as a two-stage attempt to have the best of both worlds. If the company proved unsuccessful, the bulk of the accumulated reserves would be protected. If the industry were to rebound, then the corporation would be in a position to benefit from the improved economic conditions.

Sweezy acknowledges that in normal times the $6 million cash left in the manufacturing company following the 1925 refinancing would have been satisfactory. However, because of the acute state of competition at the time, Sweezy contends that the withdrawal of almost $18 million from the manufacturing operation was a direct contradiction to Dumaine's statements relative to retaining surpluses for just such times. Sweezy proposed:

> Once the control had decided against such reinvestment, the manufacturing company was bound to fight a losing battle. The second step [the refinancing of 1927] appears dramatic simply because it so thereby carried out the logical implications of the first.[15]

In summary Sweezy states:

> Again and again they stated publicly that their primary concern was to save Amoskeag for Manchester and that the company's large reserve had been accumulated for precisely this purpose. Their actions, however, were scarcely consistent with this professed aim. As Mr. Black says: "The truth is they were pulling out their money as fast as they could and they didn't want to acknowledge it." The preservation of Amoskeag would not, of course, have solved the difficulties of New England and the cot-

ton textile industry in general. The broader question of responsibility arises out of the failure of the whole industry, not of one concern alone, to provide a tolerable existence for the hundreds of thousands of people dependent on it.[16]

When evaluating the relative merits of the criticisms of Amoskeag's financial decision making, it is important to keep in mind that they were written in the midst of the Great Depression, when primary attention was devoted to the issue of unemployment. Both hypotheses failed to address adequately the question of the fiduciary responsibility of the trustees to their stockholders. An examination of the factors leading to the 1925 refinancing has leads this writer to conclude that separation into two trusts was an attempt on the part of the trustees to fulfill their responsibilities to both their employees and their stockholders. The withdrawal of $18 million from the manufacturing operation was an indication to the stockholders, who were becoming increasingly discontent with the future outlook for the industry, that the company would only invest additional retained earnings in the manufacturing company if the future potential for profits warranted such investments. A comparison to prewar years' balance sheets indicates that more than enough cash was left in the manufacturing company. In fact, this excess cash seems to substantiate Dumaine's contention that it was left in the new trust as a potential source of funds to acquire additional New England textile manufacturers if they could be obtained at a reasonable price. The potential for the reinvestment of the $18 million back into the manufacturing trust still existed as long as the new trust remained virtually a wholly owned subsidiary.

Following the offer by Curtis, Sanger and Co. to acquire all the stock of the parent trust, the Amoskeag management was faced with what would be now called a takeover offer from a party that was explicit on its plan to liquidate the manufacturing facility. In this writer's opinion, Amoskeag's intention in its subsequent 1927 refinancing was just what the trustees stated: to allow those shareholders who desired to divest themselves of their investments at a price above the liquidation offer, while allowing the manufacturing company to be placed on its own to succeed or fail. If the company were not capable of earning a profit over and above the interest payment in the long run, then it should be liquidated. This alternative allowed the manufacturing company the opportunity to try.

III. DID AMOSKEAG ISSUE WATERED SECURITIES?

The Sabath Committee[17] charged Amoskeag with issuing watered-down securities as a result of the 1925 markup of the assets of the Amoskeag Manufacturing Company Sabath held that the subsequent refinancing of 1927 created a mechanism by which these watered securities were distributed on an unsuspecting public. The committee contended that had the firm not engaged in this process Amoskeag would have been in a stronger financial position.

Realize that the Sabath Committee was going across the country investigating bankruptcies associated with questionable public stock issues. One indicator of the committee's predisposition to the conclusion that Amoskeag was guilty of such practices can be found through an examination of the testimony of Frank G. Allen, a former governor of Massachusetts, a trustee for the bondholders during the bankruptcy procedure, and an individual with no financial ties with Amoskeag.

> **Mr. Sabath.** *Now, Governor, you were here this morning.*
>
> **Mr. Borre.** *He did not come until this afternoon.*
>
> **Mr. Allen.** *I beg your pardon. I did not come until 2:30.*
>
> **Mr. Sabath.** *This industry has been here for a long time and they started to lose money in 1924 and 1925, but it is my opinion, if they had conducted it as they did before, without falling into the clutches of these investment bankers and increased their capital from $3,000,000 to $33,000,000 at the same time, the plant would not have failed. It seems to me those interested in the plant were more interested in the speculation end than in the industrial end, which seems to have been the condition in many other sections of the country, and which I, myself, think is a grave and serious mistake. Don't you think it will be an advantage to business men if they will keep out of the clutches of these investment bankers and not seek to accumulate great wealth by floating stocks and floating bonds on the public?*
>
> **Mr. Allen.** *If that is a theoretical question and has nothing to do with——*

Mr. Sabath. *No. I am only asking you. Of course, I know you, and you don't know me, but I think you have had enough experience in public life you will give me an honest opinion. The reason I ask this is in 1929 I started a crusade in Congress to induce Congress to legislate against the stock manipulators and against this irregular manipulating and unloading on the people millions and millions of worthless securities. They issued 10 or 15 stocks, and they kept the printing presses going day and night unloading these beautiful certificates on the unsuspecting public.*

Mr. Allen. *Of course, there is no question about that. There we are of one accord on that, but it does not apply to my idea of what happened to the Amoskeag Company, because I do not know anything at all about that. But we all agreed that the manipulations there in 1928 and 1929 were unfair to the public and unfair to everybody. On the other hand, the banks have a very useful function to carry out as regards business and we have to make use of the banks, but we don't make use of that kind of bank which wants us to increase our securities until they have no value at all.*

Mr. Sabath. *Unfortunately, I find the same conditions in New England. When I first came to Boston, I actually thought I would be able to leave New England and say to New York and Chicago, "Here are people who are steady; they have not been guilty of these speculations which brought about wrack and ruin to their investors or their industries." But, unfortunately, I came across the same conditions here, where they want the last cent, and a $45,000,000 concern gets into the hands of the bankers, the very bankers who are in this thing, who immediately started to manipulate and get control of the thing under 77b, and, before anybody knew very much about it, they bought it back for $36,000,000. Where there was $77,000,000 cash on hand. They said they bought it for the bondholders, but I found out they did not buy it in for the original bondholders, but for bondholders who bought bonds for 3 cents on the dollar. Now, I think these manipulations were so unfair, some legislation should be enacted to protect the public from such transactions. Now, this company has done a splendid business for nearly 100 years. They continued doing business until this increase of capital from $3,000,000 to $36,000,000, where, immediately, these manipulators step in and bring wrack and ruin, not only to the stockholders and bondholders, but the entire* *city. I think it is an outrage, and things like that should not be condoned and that men instrumental in and behind such a movement should be taught a lesson.*

Mr. Allen. *I should want to be sure of my facts, Your Honor, before I draw any conclusion. I think those who have been responsible for the Amoskeag business will tell you, if you inquire into it, that changes in style hurt the Amoskeag Company very materially. They were, as I understand it, the largest manufacturing of fancy ginghams in the world.*

Mr. Sabath. *No doubt about it. I know that because I used to sell them and I have bought them.*

Mr. Allen. *Upon examination of the books you will find that people have not been wearing them and that hurt the Amoskeag Company*

Mr. Sabath. *If they had watched themselves in 1927, 1928, and 1929, instead of watching speculation, and, if they had devoted their knowledge, time and experience to producing merchandise that the public wanted, they could have made good goods. This concern has the finest reputation of any company in the United States.*

Mr. Allen. *I have a very high regard for these businessmen who were at the head of the Amoskeag Company, and I don't want to be a party to prejudging.*

Mr. Sabath. *I don't want to put you in the embarrassing position.*

Mr. Allen. *It is not that it is an embarrassing position. If I might give you a suggestion, I would give them their day in court to see if they have not considerable on their side.*

Mr. Sabath. *We are getting at it.*

Mr. Allen. *To see if there were not reasons which were beyond their control. It is really very effective, this ——-*

Mr. Sabath. *I am going to give them their day in court, but, when a man has been treasurer of a concern for years and, yet, he cannot tell us how much salary he has drawn and when it was increased and when it was cut, then I must ask you to concede that we* *are obliged, perhaps, to find out somewhere else and find some other methods in getting at it.*

*   **Mr. O'Malley.** *Governor, we have a letter read to the stockholders which informed the stockholders as far back as 1925 they omitted a dividend; that business was bad, and they had a $3,000,000 surplus, and then they went out and bought another company and merged the two companies. Would that indicate that business was really bad.*

*   **Mr. Allen.** *It might have been they thought they would lessen competition and make it easier for themselves by getting another unit. I suppose you have reference to Parkhill, which was an active business, as I understand it.*

*   **Mr. Sabath.** *We will not keep you.*

*   **Mr. Allen.** *I shall stay here the rest of the afternoon, but I could not come tomorrow, that is all.*

*   **Mr. Borre.** *We have another witness who cannot be here tomorrow and if we may call him out of order, I would like to call Mr. Adams if I may, now.*

*   **Mr. Sabath.** *All right, proceed.*[18]

The contention that Amoskeag was guilty of watering its securities in 1925 is proved ridiculous with the recollection that the assessment of Amoskeag's fixed assets at $33 million from the nominal $3 million carried on the books was only used to determine the relative contributions of Amoskeag and Parkhill in the new trust. All subsequent financial reports sent to stockholders exhibiting these assets were presented based on a value acknowledged by the Internal Revenue Service to appropriately reflect actual historic costs. Even Sweezy, who was critical of Amoskeag's withdrawal of cash reserves from the manufacturing operation, holds that Sabath, who was so used to seeing asset reassessments for the purpose of selling new securities, could not understand that the 1925 restatements were not excessive but only reflected updating the assets by an amount equal to undervaluations in the past.[19]

The contention that the refinancing of 1927 provided the mechanism through which these stocks could be dumped on an unsuspecting public, can as easily be dismissed after reviewing Dumaine's statements in the 1925, 1926 and 1927 annual reports of the Amoskeag Company, relative to the fact that the future of the manufacturing was so questionable that the parent company did not even place a dollar value on their 90 percent holdings in this corporation. The report also included the actual earnings of the manufacturing subsidiary during this time and continually commented on the grim outlook for the industry in the future.

When the trustees offered to exchange one share in the old trust for $52 in cash, a $40 bond in the new trust and a common share in the new trust, the shareholders knew what they would be getting. Besides $52 in cash, the investor would be getting one bond and one stock of a company handicapped by higher cost than the Southern competitors, which had a questionable future in an industry suffering from overcapacity. Investors were acquiring the securities of a firm the treasurer described as being put "upon its own responsibility to succeed or fail."[20]

IV. AMOSKEAG MANAGEMENT PRACTICES

Creamer and Coulter suggest three areas in which the ultimate demise in manufacturing in Manchester can be attributed to Amoskeag management decision making. They hold that the fact the financial decision making did not reside in Manchester kept management from fully considering the impact of their decisions on the local community. Second, they offered that the failure to move into full scale production in rayon to replace the deteriorating gingham market and the failure to spend sufficient funds in replacing textile equipment with the latest technology available in the 1920's and 1930's were contributing factors in Amoskeag's inability to counteract increased Southern competition. Finally, they said the failure to use "scientific management" as a means of combatting the lower costs of Southern manufacturers was indicative of a firm that had not kept up with the times.

Financial Decision Making in Boston

Absentee ownership and decision making from the distant Boston did not change over the 90 years of Amoskeag. The financial decision making was always centered in Boston, and the physical operation of the plants was always centered in Manchester. If anything, improvements in communication and transportation would have made the distance less of a challenge. No evidence comes forward to suspect there were inherent defects due to distance.

Even if the trustees were residents of Manchester, directors would have had to fulfill their fiduciary responsibilities to their shareholders.

The geographical location of the trustees had nothing to with altering the decisions. It is interesting to note, on the other hand, the behavior of the Boston trustees and New Hampshire bondholders in the final days prior to the liquidation. While in bankruptcy, the trustees of the corporation presented a plan to reorganize the company to continue operation. The plan gave bondholders the choice to retire each $100 bond for either one share of 5 percent first preferred stock (100 par) and 15 shares of common stock; or $50 in cash and 1/2 share of 4 percent second preferred stock (100 par). For this plan to be feasible, at least 50 percent would have to elect the first option to minimize the cash drain associated with the selection of the second option.

The Amoskeag Company, which still held some 32 percent of the bonds, was willing to accept the first alternative while many of the other bondholders, including the majority held by New Hampshire residents, elected the cash alternative. This response by New Hampshire bondholders was a contributing factor to the decision of Amoskeag to withdraw its reorganization plan and led the bankruptcy master, Mr. Black, to conclude that the corporation should be liquidated.

The trustees' loyalty to their employees and the city prevented them from expanding in the South in the late Nineteenth and early Twentieth Centuries. In the 1880's, Jefferson Coolidge considered the feasibility of building plants in the South.[21] He found a location with good waterpower. Instead, Amoskeag increased its production capacity in Manchester when it built the Jefferson Mill. A similar decision was made in 1909 under Dumaine when Amoskeag constructed the much larger Coolidge Mill. Amoskeag was well aware of the wage differential and the ability to produce at a lower cost in the South. Their loyalty to Manchester was the sole determining factor not to pursue this course of action.

Capital Expenditures in the 1920's and 1930's

On the issue of letting the equipment become obsolete, Creamer and Coulter fail to recognize the difference between a cause and an effect. It is true that in the last ten to fifteen years of its operation Amoskeag did not spend as much on repairs and new equipment as it had in previous years. But these decisions, as in all past decisions, were based on whether the investment in equipment would be profitable. Following the end of the war there was substantial overcapacity. New investments would not be warranted beyond those required to keep currently used equipment operating efficiently. If and when the balance between supply and demand became more normal, the increased investments in new equipment would be forthcoming. In the interim, Amoskeag was operating in the short run, attempting to minimize losses. As long as it could cover variable costs and put something toward fixed costs, it would continue operations. But such a condition does not warrant new investments.

Creamer and Coulter would argue that the investment in new equipment would have had the effect of making Amoskeag more cost competitive and, therefore, should have been decided even in the current market conditions. Such a conclusion fails to recognize the difference between decision making in the long run and decision making in the short run. To entice manufacturers to invest additional capital, they must see the potential for future sales to cover the cost of labor and materials, and, over time, to return a surplus over the cost of the equipment. When Amoskeag examined the future potential market for its goods together with the cost associated with its manufacturing, the company could not project profits from additional capital investments. If labor costs were equal to those in the South, then a satisfactory return could have been earned on those potential investments in new equipment, and Amoskeag would have undertaken those projects.

However, when making decisions on currently existing capacity, one is operating in the short run. While the firm obviously would have preferred to make a profit, it would continue operating those portions of its business that covered the incremental cost associated with its production. Under such conditions, investments in equipment would be kept to a minimum.

The Use of Scientific Management

The final point in which Creamer and Coulter criticized management of Amoskeag was in use of time and motion studies to increase production. At this point, Creamer and Coulter contradict themselves relative to an example they used to illustrate the condition of the equipment in the later years. They cite examples of employee complaints that equipment was not adequate to support the increased output per worker requested by management. Creamer and Coulter contend that to generate the full effect of this increased output required updating equipment. The issue again becomes one of the difference between short-run and long-run decision making. The ultimate conclusion as to whether these investments in the 1920's and 1930's that did not take place would have been able to sustain themselves requires an analysis of the relative costs of Amoskeag and the growing Southern competition. This writer believes that the cost differential was not one of many contributing factors to Amoskeag's eventual demise, but that it was **the only** factor.

V. THE IMPACT OF SOUTHERN COMPETITION

Creamer and Coulter devote a considerable amount of their work to the wage differential between New England and Southern manufacturers. They also vividly depict the growth in Southern output. They fail to realize the overall dominance of this fact on the ultimate fate of production in Manchester. While they point to the tremendous increase in capacity in the South, the relative inelastic market demand for a homogeneous product, and the significant cost differential in labor, they fail to conclude that either New England firms had to obtain substantial wage concessions or face eventual bankruptcy. To assume that the utilization of cash reserves for further investments in the latest equipment, when the same equipment was available to the Southern manufacturers, would somehow overcome Amoskeag's labor cost disadvantage, is naive, at best. While most critics attribute the demise of Amoskeag to the financial restructuring of 1925 and 1927, this writer attributes the ultimate bankruptcy to the final outcome of Amoskeag's attempt to lower wages in 1922.

Wage Differentials and the 1922 Strike

In the years preceding the outbreak of the World War I,

management was becoming increasingly concerned with the growth of production in the South. While New England firms continued to be prosperous, the amount of their profits suffered from the output of lower cost Southern producers. The increased demand that resulted from the outbreak of the war proved to be a mixed blessing. The immediate result was unprecedented profits on the part of Amoskeag, but, even larger profits were earned by the Southern manufacturers, providing the latter with both increased incentives and the financial resources to expand. While these Southern firms obviously realized that further expansion after the war would produce a situation of overcapacity, they were well aware of their labor cost advantage. As long as this advantage continued, they would be successful in driving their New England counterparts out of business.

One could hypothesize that Amoskeag, with its vast size, quality reputation and financial resources, could use predatory price cutting to drive the Southern producers out of business. This would have proved to be an unwise strategy for three reasons.

First, while Amoskeag was the largest cotton textile producer in the world, it supplied only 3 percent of the national market. It did not dominate the industry.

Second, because it had higher production costs than its Southern competitors, Amoskeag would have had to inflict greater losses on itself in the process of eliminating its competition. Such a situation makes the potential for success highly unlikely.

Third, and most important, even if cash reserves prior to the refinancing of 1925 and 1927 were adequate to succeed in this endeavor, once Amoskeag returned to full cost pricing, it would be met by new entrants in the South. The obvious alternative of establishing production facilities in the South would have insured Amoskeag's position in the future world of textiles, but it would not have done anything to maintain production in Manchester.

The one strategy that Amoskeag and other New England producers could have pursued was to have brought local labor costs in line with those of the South. The original geographical superiority of New England was its cheap and plentiful waterpower. By the end of the war, Amoskeag's production had grown to the point that waterpower could not adequately meet its total energy needs. In addition, advances in coal generated power made it a cost effective substitute for waterpower. Southern mills could purchase coal at a rate equal to or below the North. At the same time, New England mills faced higher transportation costs for raw materials, higher local taxes and higher labor costs. Of all the diseconomies, the labor cost differential was, by far, the most important.

During the years 1900 to 1922, mill employees shared in the prosperity of the corporation by gaining both substantial hourly wage increases and a decrease in the workweek. By 1922, the hourly wage differential between the North and South was 30 to 40 percent. In addition, the Southern mills operated between 55 to 60 hours a week in contrast to the 48 hours in the North. Even after factoring in some reduction in productivity for the longer workweek, the net result would be a substantially lower overhead cost per labor hour, further enhancing the cost advantage of Southern manufacturers.

Under the assumption that a significant labor rate concession was necessary for the survival of Amoskeag and other New England textile firms, one might examine how an alternative strategy could have been more successful. In the early days of the 1922 strike, the union continually pointed to high Amoskeag profits. If New England manufacturers had waited until 1923 or 1924 when their earnings reflected lower profits or losses, they might have found less work opposition to wage concessions. On the other hand, every year that New England manufacturers delayed this attempt to bring equity in the rates of pay between the North and South resulted in more and more capacity being built in the South. In retrospect, however, the records show that post 1922 attempts were not successful, either.

Amoskeag management took a powerful position on the workweek for two reasons. First, it was a way of lowering the average fixed cost of operation by spreading fixed costs over more output. Second, it was a way of mitigating the effect of the hourly wage cut on the take-home pay. As stated in "A Letter to The People of New Hampshire Regarding Amoskeag," the reduction of 20 percent in the hourly wage rate combined with an hour increase of 12.5 percent resulted in a net reduction of 10 percent in weekly wages.

The union was opposed to the longer workweek, but acknowledged a willingness to discuss a wage decrease early in the strike. In light of the eventual loss of the hourly wage issues by the company and the fact that due to the cost disadvantage the firm never operated at near capacity following the strike, one could ask whether a compromise resulting in a 10 percent reduction in wages and no increase in hours might not have been a viable alternative that would have left both parties better off. The employees would have left with the same net reduction in take-home pay as the original company plan without incurring the increase in working hours. The company would have been left with some economy in labor cost that did not depend on operating at capacity. An even more important issue is what would have been the response on the part of Southern manufacturers to a permanent drop in the rate of pay up North. The fact that the cost of living was significantly lower in the South might have meant that wage decreases in the North would have been met with similar decreases in the South. A review of the history following the strike up until Amoskeag's bankruptcy in 1936 seems to substantiate this belief. If this is true, then the demise of textile production in the North was inevitable.

The Impact of Labor Cost Differences in Profitability

The author has emphatically stated that the only significant factor that caused the demise of the Amoskeag Manufacturing Company was the difference in labor cost between the North and the South. It is crucial to understand that because of the relatively inelastic demand for the product and low brand loyalty, it was not the actual wage rate paid as much as it was the *difference* in the wage rates. To address whether Amoskeag Manufacturing Company was a viable firm during the period of time that the new trust was formed until the preferred stock was refunded for cash and the bond issue, Table II illustrates the average annual earnings with actual labor costs. The table then contrasts this performance with what the earnings would have been assuming total labor cost was 20 percent lower under varying output assumptions. For these latter calculations, it was assumed that the firms would not experience any savings in other average costs as output expanded. Even if Amoskeag could not sell additional output, it would have seen an average loss of $799,000 become a profit of $1,210,000 if it had experienced a 20 percent reduction in

TABLE II

COMPARISON OF ACTUAL AVERAGE EARNINGS IN 1926-27
With Earning Potential Assuming Labor Costs Equal To South

$1,000s

	Actual Labor Cost	Labor Cost at 80% of Actual Cost at Alternative Output Levels			
Output as a Percent of Capacity	60%	60%	70%	80%	90%
Total Revenue	$29,298	$29,298	$34,181	$39,064	$43,947
Labor Costs	$10,042	$ 8,034	$ 9,373	$10,712	$12,051
Non-Labor Costs	20,054	20,054	23,396	26,739	30,081
Total Costs of Manufacturing	$30,076	$28,088	$32,769	$37,451	$42,132
Earnings Before Preferred Dividends	($ 798)	$ 1,210	$ 1,412	$ 1,613	$ 1,815
Preferred Dividends	1,590	1,590	1,590	1,590	1,590
Earnings Available for Common Stock	($ 2,388)	($ 380)	($ 178)	$ 23	$ 225
Earnings Per Share	($ 6.55)	($ 1.04)	($ 0.49)	$ 0.06	$ 0.62

labor cost. If the company could sell additional output, the average annual profits would grow to be as much as $1,815,000. Regardless of the assumption one makes on the level of output selected, it is obvious that the labor cost savings would be more then sufficient to make Amoskeag a profitable corporation. However, unless the volume could be increased substantially, the profits would not be sufficient to cover the dividends on the preferred stock and thus there would be little or no earning for the common stock. While it is true that the preferred dividend did not have to be paid in a case where the earnings were not present, they did have to be paid before any common dividends could be paid.

In the 1927 refinancing, the preferred stock was retired for cash and an issue of 6 percent bonds. The refinancing substantially reduced the total payments that would have had to be paid before the common stock would have any earnings. Prior to the restructuring, the preferred dividends amounted to $1,590,000. Since cash was used to finance part of the retirement, a substantially smaller bond issue carried interest obligations of only $560,000. Table III prepares a similar calculation to the previous table for the five years following the bond issue.

TABLE III
COMPARISON OF ACTUAL AVERAGE EARNINGS IN 1928-32
With Earning Potential Assuming Labor Costs Equal To South

$1,000s

	Actual Labor Cost	Labor Cost at 90% of Actual Cost at Alternative Output Levels			
Output as a Percent of Capacity	60%	60%	70%	80%	90%
Total Revenue	$21,030	$21,030	$24,535	$28,040	$31,345
Labor Costs	$ 6,403	$ 5,763	$ 6,723	$ 7,684	$ 8,644
Non-Labor Costs	14,662	14,662	17,106	19,549	21,993
Total Costs of Manufacturing	$21,662	$20,425	$23,829	$27,233	$30,637
Earnings Before Bond Interest	($ 35)	$ 605	$ 706	$ 807	$ 908
Bond Interest	560	560	560	560	560
Earnings Available for Common Stock	($ 695)	$ 45	$ 146	$ 247	$ 348
Earnings Per Share	($ 1.57)	$ 0.12	$ 0.38	$ 0.65	$ 0.92

Because negotiations with labor resulted in some movement toward equality in wages with the South, this analysis illustrates the impact of only a 10 percent savings in labor costs. The results are similar to those demonstrated in the previous table. In reference to the magnitude of earnings, the refinancing caused the potential earnings available to common stockholders to increase. It should be reemphasized that this potential improvement to common stockholders was partially a result of the retirement of a portion of the preferred stock issue for cash rather than the substitution of the remaining portion of preferred stock with bonds. The same result could have been reached by retiring half of the preferred stock and leaving the remainder as preferred stock rather than substituting bonds. However, as mentioned earlier in this chapter in the section on the 1927 refinancing, Amoskeag had to devise a plan that would prevent an unfriendly takeover with the intention of liquidating the mills. The simple retirement of half of the preferred stock issue would not have met the need.

The figures presented here are hypothetical because the proposed lowering of the relative wage rate never really materialized. Even as the country went deeper and deeper into the depression and wages across the country dropped, the South maintained a labor cost advantage at least equal to the 10 to 20 percent estimated in these tables. The results presented show the potential rewards to be gained had Amoskeag been successful in eliminating the labor cost disadvantage. Considering this fact, we gain a better understanding of Amoskeag's past decisions relative to the strong position that it took in the strike of 1922, the subsequent refinancing in 1925 and 1927, and the curtailment in investment in equipment in the last few years of the corporation.

This author's conclusion is that there are few aspects that actually can be discovered or deduced to criticize the management of Amoskeag for its decisions in the twentieth century. New England mills were faced with increasing competition by producers in another section of the country who had substantial cost advantages. With careful and intense scrutiny, there is little else that Dumaine or Amoskeag's management could have done in its unrelenting attempt to save the textile industry in the City of Manchester.

Epilogue

Following Amoskeag's decision to withdraw its plan for reorganization, the company was declared legally insolvent by the in the Federal District Court on July 21, 1936. In a subsequent decision, the bonds of the Amoskeag Manufacturing Company held by the Amoskeag Company were placed subordinate to all other bonds. In effect the court agreed with the petition of Mrs. Eliza Leland and financier Frederick H. Prince that all other bondholders should be paid in full prior to the Amoskeag Company receiving one cent.

Dumaine was named one of three co-trustees of the bankruptcy with W. Parker Straw, Amoskeag's former agent and Joseph F. Carney, the former head of the New Deal's Reconstruction Finance Committee for New England.

Shortly thereafter, a group of Manchester men organized Amoskeag Industries, a company that wished to purchase the mills prior to a scheduled bankruptcy auction. Five hundred thousand dollars was raised in cash. Public Service of New Hampshire, the local public utility, offered $2 million for the power plants and water rights. An additional $2 million was loaned by the various Manchester savings banks. While the Manchester group hoped to attract potential textile firms with bargain basement purchase prices, they also hoped to attract a diversified group of non-textile investors wishing to take advantage of Manchester's empty factories and abundant labor force.

While the $5 million was probably less than what would have been raised by the auction, Dumaine and the other trustees agreed to the purchase plan. Their primary reason was to prevent the equipment that would have been auctioned off from finding its way to Southern mills. The sale to Manchester interests that intended to lease or sell portions of the various mills with its equipment in tact provided the greatest opportunity for maximum reemployment of Manchester's labor force.

Shortly after the takeover of the mills, the principals of Amoskeag Industries approached Dumaine to run the textile operations. He refused. Three possible reasons emerge:

One is that he felt he was too old at the age of seventy to start over.

Two, he was warned in the Sabath hearing that it would not be looked on favorably if he were to regain control of the mills.

Three, he may have felt betrayed by Manchester interests.

Many of the parties involved with the financing of Amoskeag Industries were among the Manchester bondholders who were reluctant in their support of Amoskeag Manufacturing Company's refinancing.

While Amoskeag Industries was moderately successful in finding firms willing to take advantage of the low-cost mill sites, it is questionable whether the employment grew as fast as it would have been under the manufacturing company's proposed refinancing.

Based on the proceeds from the sale of the mills to Amoskeag Industries and the subsequent liquidation of current assets, Amoskeag Manufacturing Company was able to pay off all debts, including those bonds held by Amoskeag Company. In response to the final filing of the liquidation, Referee Arthur Black, the bankruptcy master, commented, "Our difficulty comes from the fact that we never before had a case which paid creditors in full!" The surplus was distributed to the shareholders of Amoskeag Manufacturing Company. stock in the form of a liquidation dividend.

Dumaine continued as treasurer of Amoskeag Company, the holding company, until 1939, at which time he was named president. This was a reflection of the reorganization of authority inasmuch as the president became the chief executive officer, while the position of treasurer was changed from chief executive officer to chief financial officer. He remained as president until 1946, when he became chairman of the board, a title he held until his death in 1951. Dumaine was succeeded as treasurer and then president by his son, F.C. (Buck) Dumaine, Jr.

Following the liquidation of the mills, the holding company invested heavily in various railroads, including the Bangor and Aroostook, the Boston and Maine, the Delaware and Hudson, and the Maine Central. In 1948, Dumaine gained control of the New Haven.

Two years after Dumaine's death, Amoskeag Company reentered the textile field by purchasing a substantial interest in Fieldcrest Mills from Marshall Fields. In addition, the company at one time owned Avis, Inc., Fanny Farmer Candy Shops, Inc. and Westville Homes Corp.

In the early 1990's, Amoskeag Company owned 3,606,400 shares of Fieldcrest's class B common stock, which while representing only 30 percent of Fieldcrest's total outstanding common stock, controlled 80.7 percent of the aggregate votes. On November 24, 1993, Fieldcrest completed a tender offer for all of the outstanding shares of Amoskeag Company. As a result of the merger, Amoskeag, the former parent company, became a wholly owned subsidiary of Fieldcrest, the former subsidiary company, and Amoskeag Company, first incorporated in 1931, went out of existence as a separate company.

NOTES

<u>Preface</u>

1. "Unpublished History of the Amoskeag Manufacturing Company", Author Unknown (Dumaine Files).

2. Daniel Creamer and Charles W. Coulter, Labor and the Shut-Down of the Amoskeag Textile MillsWorks Project Administration, National Research Project, No. L-5, Philadelphia, Pa., 1939.

3. Wayman, "Unpublished Notes on Dumaine's Diary," (Dumaine Files).

4. Brown, George Waldo, The Amoskeag Manufacturing CompanyManchester, N. H.: Amoskeag Manufacturing Company Print Shop, 1915.

<u>Post Script</u>

1. Wayman, Dorothy G., Dumaine of New England, unpublishedmanuscript, 1958.

2. Wayman

3. Wayman

4. Wayman

<u>Chapter I</u>

1. "Amoskeag Manufacturing Company," Stories of Certain Massachusetts Industries, reprinted from the Boston Globe, 1915.

2. Hareven, Tamara & Langenbach, Randolph, Amoskeag, Pantheon Books, New York, N.Y., 1978.

3. Hareven & Langenbach, p. 332.

4. Hareven & Langenbach, p. 347-348.

5. District Court of the United States, District of Massachusetts, Amoskeag Manufacturing Corporation Bankruptcy Hearing No. 58.599

6. Alan R. Sweezy, "The Amoskeag Manufacturing Company", Quarterly Journal of Economics, Vol. LII, No. 3 (May 1938).

7. Adolph J. Sabath, Chairman, Investigation of Real Estate Bondholders' Reorganizations, U. S. Congress, House of Representatives, Public Hearings Before a Subcommittee of the Senate, Sept. 30, Oct. 1 & 2, 1936.

8. Daniel Creamer and Charles W. Coulter, Labor and the Shut-Down of the Amoskeag Textile MillsWorks Project Administration, National Research Project, No. L-5, Philadelphia, Pa., 1939.

9. Saunders, Dero A., "Frederic Dumaine: Upstreaming the Profits", <u>Forbes</u>, July 13 1987, p. 258-262.

10, "Boot Hill, Tales form the Corporate Graveyard," Audacity, Spring 1993, p. 63.

Chapter X

1. Daniel Creamer and Charles W. Coulter, Labor and the Shut-Down of the Amoskeag Textile MillsWorks Project Administration, National Research Project, No. L-5, Philadelphia, Pa., 1939.

2. Manchester Mills, Treasurer's Report 1905

3. Lewis Dexter, History of the Stark Division of the International Cotton Mills Manchester, N.H., 1921.

4. District Court of the United States, District of Massachusetts, Amoskeag Manufacturing Corporation Bankruptcy Hearing No. 58.599

5. Creamer and Coulter, p. 9.

6. Creamer and Coulter.

7. Alan R. Sweezy, "The Amoskeag Manufacturing Company", Quarterly Journal of Economics, Vol. LII, No. 3 (May 1938).

8. Amoskeag Manufacturing Company, Annual Report, 1920.

9. Amoskeag Manufacturing Company, May 31, 1924 Letter to Shareholders.

10. Amoskeag Company, Annual Report, 1925.

11. Amoskeag Company, Annual Report, 1925.

12. Amoskeag Company, Notice to Shareholders, n.d.

13. Amoskeag Company, Nov. 21, 1927 Offer to Shareholders.

14. Amoskeag Company, Nov. 21, 1927 Offer to Shareholders.

15. Sweezy, p. 493.

16. Sweezy, p. 512.

17. Adolph J. Sabath, Chairman, Investigation of Real Estate Bondholders' Reorganizations, U. S. Congress, House of Representatives, Public Hearings Before a Subcommittee of the Senate, Sept. 30, Oct. 1 & 2, 1936.

18. Sabath, p. 46-48.

19. Sweezy, p. 492.

20. Amoskeag Company, Nov. 21, Offer to Shareholders.

21. Amoskeag Manufacturing Company, Annual Report, 1935.

BIBLIOGRAPHY

Amory Mills, Corporate Records, 1879 - 1906.

Amoskeag Company, Annual Reports, 1906 - 1936.

Amoskeag Company, Corporate Records, 1856 - 1938.

Amoskeag Company, Notice to Shareholders, n.d.

Amoskeag Company, Nov. 21, 1927, Offer to Shareholders.

Amoskeag Manufacturing Company, Annual Reports, 1927 - 1936.

Amoskeag Manufacturing Company, Corporate Records, 1925 - 1936.

"Amoskeag Manufacturing Company," Stories of Certain Massachusetts Industries, reprinted from the Boston Globe, 1915.

"Boot Hill, Tales form the Corporate Graveyard," Audacity, Spring 1993, p. 63.

Brown, George Waldo, The Amoskeag Manufacturing Company Manchester, N. H.: Amoskeag Manufacturing Company Print Shop, 1915.

Clark, John B., History of Manchester, Manchester, N. H.: Mirror Office, 1875.

Creamer, Daniel and Charles W. Coulter, Labor and the Shut-Down of the Amoskeag Textile Mills, Works Project Administration, National Research Project, No. L-5, Philadelphia, Pa., 1939.

Dexter, Lewis, History of the Stark Division of the International Cotton Mills, Manchester, N. H., 1921.

District Court of the United States, District of Massachusetts, Amoskeag Manufacturing Company Bankruptcy Hearings No. 58,599., 1936.

Dumaine, Frederic C., Personal Files of the Treasurer of the Amoskeag Manufacturing Company, Manchester Historic Association.

Manchester Union, 1922-1937.

History of the Amoskeag Strike Author Unknown, Manchester, N.H.: Amoskeag Manufacturing Company Print Shop, 1924.

Langdon Mills, Corporate Records, 1857 - 1887.

Manchester Mills, Corporate Records, 1904 - 1906.

Sabath, Adolph J., Chairman, Investigation of Real Estate Bondholders' Reorganizations U. S. Congress, House of Representatives, Public Hearing Before a Subcommittee of the Select Committee, Sept. 30, Oct. 1 & 2, 1934.

Sweezy, Alan R., "The Amoskeag Manufacturing Company," Quarterly Journal of Economics Vol. LII, No. 3, (May 1938).

Tilden, Leonard E., "New England Textile Strike," Monthly Labor Review Vol. XVI, (May 1923).

"Unpublished History of the Amoskeag Manufacturing Company," Author Unknown (Dumaine Files).

Wayman, "Unpublished Notes on Dumaines Diary," (Dumaine Files).

Wayman, Dorothy G., Dumaine of New England, unpublished manuscript, 1958.

Chronological Summary

of the

Amoskeag Manufacturing Company

1805 Benjamin Pichard began manufacturing in his mill at Amoskeag in the fall of the year.

1810 State Legislature granted at act of incorporation to the "Amoskeag Cotton and Woolen Manufacturing Company."

1822 Olney Robinson purchased the manufacturing plant at Amoskeag

1825 Mill property at Amoskeag Falls passed into possession of Misters. Slater, Dean, Tiffany, Sayles, Pitcher and Gay.

1826 "Bell Mill" built.

1827 "Island Mill" built.

1831 "Amoskeag Manufacturing Company" incorporated.

1834 First dividend declared.

1835 Amoskeag began construction of canals on the east side of the river.

1837 William Amory elected treasurer.

1838 Stark Manufacturing Company incorporated.

1839 First Stark Mill completed, beginning production on the east side of the river. Employed daughters of yankee farm families. Women lived in company built boardinghouses.

1839 Manchester Mills chartered.

1840   Island Mill destroyed by fire.

1840   First Irish operators in Manchester began work in the Stark Mill.

1841   Amoskeag completed construction of its first mill on the east side of the river.

1844   First Manchester mill completed.

1849   Amoskeag built its first locomotive. A total of 232 would be built over the next ten years, at which time the business was sold to the Manchester Locomotive Works.

1851   Amoskeag awarded first medal for superiority of goods at the London World's Fair.

1856   Ezekiel A. Straw chosen as agent.

1859   Amoskeag built its first steam fire engine. A total of 550 would be built over the next eighteen years, at which time this business was also sold to the Manchester Locomotive Works.

1860   Langdon mill incorporated.

1864   First French Canadians working in mills.

1866   F.C. Dumaine born March 6 in Hadley Massachusetts.

1872   Herman Straw, son of E.A. Straw employed at Amoskeag.

1874   Langdon mall organized.

1874   Manchester mills sold at auction.

1876   T. Jefferson Coolidge replaces William Amory as treasurer of Amoskeag.

1878   Christopher Dumaine, F.C.'s father, dies. F.C. begins work at Henry Pettingall drygoods store.

1879   Thomas Livingston replaces E.A. Straw as agent at Amoskeag.

1879   Amory Manufacturing Company organized.

1880 F.C. begins working for Amoskeag as an office boy at $3.00 per week under Lucius Manulius Sargent and T. Jefferson Coolidge.

1885 Herman Straw, second of three generations of Straws, becomes agent at Amoskeag.

1886 Jefferson mill built even though management knew labor costs were lower in the South.

1887 Langdon mill merged into Amory mill.

1888 F.C. moves to Boston in order to go to night school, while working at Amoskeag during the day.

1889 F.C. sent to Manchester to learn the manufacturing end of the business.

1891 F.C. brought back to Boston as a buyer.

1893 F.C. moved to selling and accounting department.

1895 F.C. marries Bessie Thomas, April 13.

1896 Charles A. Amory, son of William Amory, replaces Coolidge as treasurer of Amoskeag.

1897 Mary Dumaine, F.C. & Bessie's first child, born April 19.

1898 F.C. appointed treasurer of Amory Manufacturing Company.

1900 Elizabeth Dumaine, second child, born January 3.

1900 Cordelia Dumaine, F.C.'s mother dies, June 23.

1901 Harriet Dumaine, third child, born March 12.

1901 Stark Mill sold to U.S. Cotton Duck trust.

1902 F.C. (Buck) Dumaine, Jr., fourth child, born September 5.

1902 F.C. becomes involved with management of Fore River Ship & Engine Company, Quincy Massachusetts.

1903 Manchester Mills acquired by T. Jefferson Coolidge. F.C. appointed treasurer and given responsibility for refurbishing the mills.

1905 F.C. appointed treasurer of Amoskeag.

1905 Amory and Manchester mills acquired and merged into the Amoskeag Manufacturing Company,

1907 Cordelia Dumaine, fifth child, born February 17.

1908 F.C. becomes a director of the Boston and Maine Railroad.

1908 F.C. becomes a director of the Old Colony Trust Company.

1909 F.C. becomes president of the Boston Railroad Holding Company.

1909 Coolidge Mill built.

1910 Christopher Dumaine, sixth child, born April 6.

1911 Amoskeag reorganized as a voluntary trust.

1912 Thomas Park Dumaine, seventh and last child, born August 21. Thomas Park's name was later legally changed to Pierre.

1912 Dumaine establishes Amoskeag employee welfare system: clinics, dental care, visiting nurses, technical school, social clubs, stock purchase plan and building lots for residential houses.

1914 Year of maximum physical output by Amoskeag mills.

1914 Bessie, F.C.'s wife, becomes active in Women's Suffrage Movement. On May 2 she carried flag in Boston parade.

1914 Fore River Ship & Engine Company sold to Bethlehem Steel.

1916 F.C. and Bessie separate. Bessie moves to Cambridge. The four oldest children remain with F.C. The three youngest live with their mother.

1918 Buck Dumaine sent to Amoskeag mills for a summer job between academic years.

1919 Amoskeag profits reach all time high associated with war time production.

1919 F.C. and Bessie divorce.

1920 Dumaine's Trust formed for F.C.'s children and grandchildren.

1920 Parker Straw succeeds his father Herman as agent at Amoskeag in June. He was the third generation of Straws to hold that position.

1921 Amoskeag's earnings of $1,273,000 fall short of dividend requirements of $2,524,000 resulting in a reduction in surplus of $1,251,000.

1922 Amoskeag's nine-month strike

1923 F.C. takes over management of reorganized Waltham Watch Company.

1923 F.C. marries Louise (Weesie) Gould on December 3.

1924 Amoskeag suffers a $2,851,000 loss before payment of dividend.

1924 Waltham Watch strike

1925 Amoskeag reorganized into Amoskeag Company, a holding company, and Amoskeag Manufacturing Company, an operating company, to appease stockholders concerned that future losses would erode past profits accumulated by Amoskeag.

1927 Offer by Curtis, Sanger & Co. of New York, to purchase Amoskeag companies with intent of closing mills and liquidating property, refused by directors.

1927 Dumaine refinances manufacturing company with intent of preventing liquidation of Manchester facilities by subsequent corporate raiders. More than two thirds of Amoskeag Company stockholders accepted offer to swap their shares of the holding company for $52 in cash, a $40 bond of the manufacturing company and a share of the manufacturing company.

1927 Beginning of a five-year period during which Amoskeag was to operate at a level of approximately 50 percent of capacity in an attempt of minimize operating losses.

1928 In July, Dumaine meets with Arthur Vining Davis, president of Aluminum Corporation of America, in an attempt to convince Davis to construct an aluminum plant on the Merrimack, thereby providing jobs and allow Amoskeag to partially liquidate mills. Davis concludes water power was not sufficient to justify construction of aluminum plant.

1929 Parker Straw, the third of three generations of Straws that served as agents, resigns on January 18.

1929 Because labor agreed to accept wage reductions Amoskeag was able to successfully bid on profitable sales contracts. Profit of $1,066,000 earned for the year. One third of profits was paid out as a bonus to labor in the form of savings deposits in various Manchester banks.

1930 Merrimack River Savings Bank, one of the banks authorized to receive employees' bonuses, closed. Amoskeag covers loss to employees who still had bonus deposited in the bank.

1935 In February, Dumaine spoke in front of the Cotton Textile Code Authority urging for equality of wages between the North and the South under the National Recovery Act.

1935 In the spring Amoskeag began process of closing mills. By September most production rooms were closed and employment was below 1,000 workers. Dumaine emphasized that workers must accept competitive wages and production for Amoskeag to reopen on a profitable basis.

1935 In March Amoskeag razed Langdon Mill No. 1 and two smaller mills in an attempt to lower property taxes.

1935 On June 6, Amoskeag sold Mill No. 12, which had an
      original construction cost of $164,000, for $17,500.

1935 Dumaine meets with Reconstruction Finance Committee, a
      part of Roosevelt's New Deal, attempting to seek funds to
      reopen mills.

1935 On November 12, the Textile Advisory Board, a commit-
      tee appointed by New Hampshire Governor Styles Bridges
      and headed by Bishop John Peterson, submitted its report,
      calling for greater production efficiency, further tax relief,
      and greater cooperation between Management and labor.
      The committee opposed Dumaine's position on the
      necessity of wage cuts.

1935 December 24, Amoskeag, whose bonds were in default,
      filed for protection under the bankruptcy act while it
      attempted to restructure its financing in order to reopen the
      mills.

1936 March 9, Amoskeag Manufacturing Company submits plan
      for refinancing to reopen the mills. Proposal required a
      majority of bondholders to trade in their bonds for pre-
      ferred stock.

1936 March 11-12, the Merrimack River overflowed Amoskeag
      Dam wiping out bridges and causing $2.5 million dollars in
      damage to the mills. Amoskeag Manufacturing Company
      was still willing to go along with refinancing plan.

1936 March 17, Amoskeag Company, the holding company,
      which owned 32 percent of the manufacturing company,
      was willing to accept the manufacturing company's reorgani-
      zation plan even after assessing the impact of the flood.

1936 March 24, Dumaine met with Manchester bondholders,
      who were undecided whether to accept the refinancing or
      to try and force bankruptcy.

1936 April 6 court hearing on reorganization. Manchester bond
      holders of $1.1 million bonds, critical for the refinancing to
      be successful, still undecided.

1936 April 16, Dumaine meets again with Manchester bondholders.

1936 May, Manchester and Boston newspapers state Manchester bondholders willing to go along with refinancing.

1936 June 7, date that "Buck" Dumaine states that Manchester bondholders reneged on agreement to go along with refinancing.

1936 June 9, Amoskeag Manufacturing Company withdraws reorganization plan since, "...the assets of the company will be depleted by reason of the fact that so many bondholders have elected to withdraw cash...particularly in New Hampshire..."

1936 July 21, the Amoskeag Manufacturing Company declared insolvent in Federal District Court. Dumaine, Joseph Carney of Reconstruction Financial Committee, and W. Parker Straw were named co-trustees of the bankruptcy.

1936 Manchester citizens formed Amoskeag Industries to purchase the mills and related property. They subscribed $500,000 in cash, obtained $2.5 million from the Manchester Traction Light and Power, for the power plant and water rights. The remaining $2 million paid to Amoskeag Manufacturing was loaned by Manchester savings banks.

1936 Following the closing of the mills, Amoskeag Company, the holding company, invested heavily in railroads.

1939 "Buck" Dumaine replaces F.C. as treasurer of Amoskeag Company, the holding company. F.C. assumes the position of president.

1940 February 1, final summary of bankruptcy of the manufacturing company. All creditors paid in full.

1946 F.C. retires as president of Amoskeag Company but continues as chairman of the board until his death.

1951 F.C. Dumaine died, May 27.

Index

ABOUT THE AUTHOR

Arthur Kenison was raised in Manchester while the city was still recovering from the economic impact of the closing of the Amoskeag mills. He graduated from Saint Anselm College in 1963. Dr. Kenison holds advanced degrees from Columbia University, the University of New Hampshire and Boston University. Professor Kenison, a long-time member of the faculty of Saint Anselm College, is a highly respected and sought after consultant in the field of forensic economics. He resides with his wife Jeanne in Amoskeag Place, one of the many complexes of mill housing built by Amoskeag.

As this book went to press, Dr. Kenison was well engrossed in editing his next book, *Dumaine of New England,* based on oral history, personal Dumaine files and galley proofs of a book-in-progress started in the 1950's by the late Dorothy G. Wayman.